Bella Coco's
CROCHET STITCH LIBRARY

DEDICATION

To my husband Anthony and my girls, Ella and Everleigh;
I love you with all of my heart.

To my parents, who have always been my biggest cheerleaders;
I love you and I cannot thank you enough.

To my Dad up in heaven; everything I do is in hope I would've
made you proud. I love you and miss you.

ACKNOWLEDGEMENTS

Huge thanks to my editor, Emily Adam, who I've had the
pleasure of working with again; thank you for your kindness
and guidance.

Thank you to Nicola White, Emma Carter, Jacqui Fisher
(aka Mummy Coco) and Emily Reiter for your contribution
towards this book. I really do have the best team!

Finally, thank you to every single person who purchased
my first book and enabled me to write a second!
Your support means the world.

Bella Coco's
CROCHET STITCH LIBRARY

My Top 100 Stitches, Borders and Motifs

Sarah-Jayne Fragola

SEARCH PRESS

CONTENTS

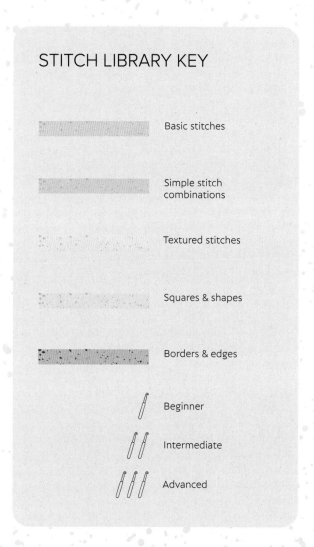

STITCH LIBRARY KEY

Basic stitches

Simple stitch combinations

Textured stitches

Squares & shapes

Borders & edges

Beginner

Intermediate

Advanced

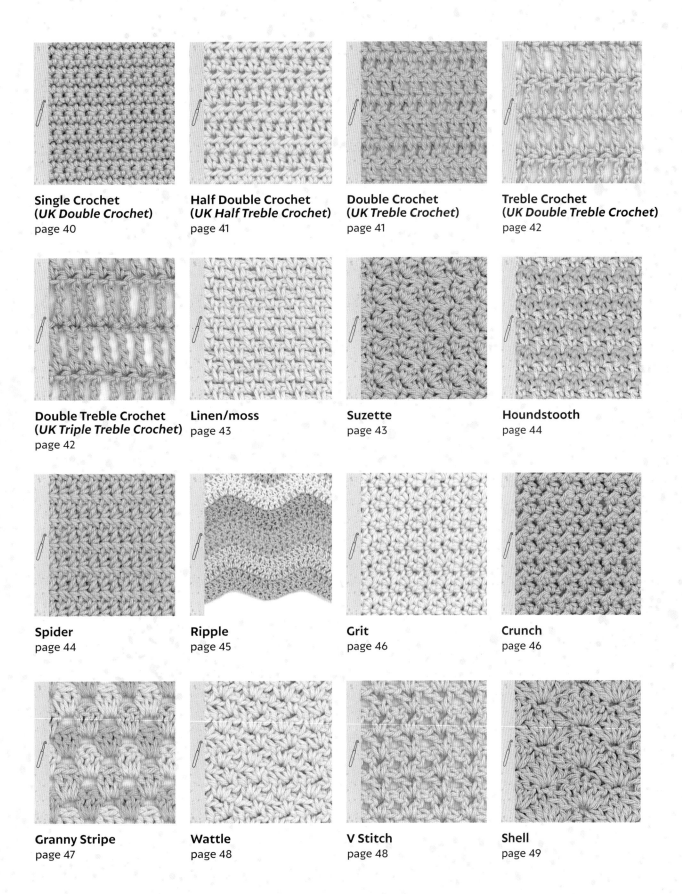

Single Crochet
(*UK Double Crochet*)
page 40

Half Double Crochet
(*UK Half Treble Crochet*)
page 41

Double Crochet
(*UK Treble Crochet*)
page 41

Treble Crochet
(*UK Double Treble Crochet*)
page 42

Double Treble Crochet
(*UK Triple Treble Crochet*)
page 42

Linen/moss
page 43

Suzette
page 43

Houndstooth
page 44

Spider
page 44

Ripple
page 45

Grit
page 46

Crunch
page 46

Granny Stripe
page 47

Wattle
page 48

V Stitch
page 48

Shell
page 49

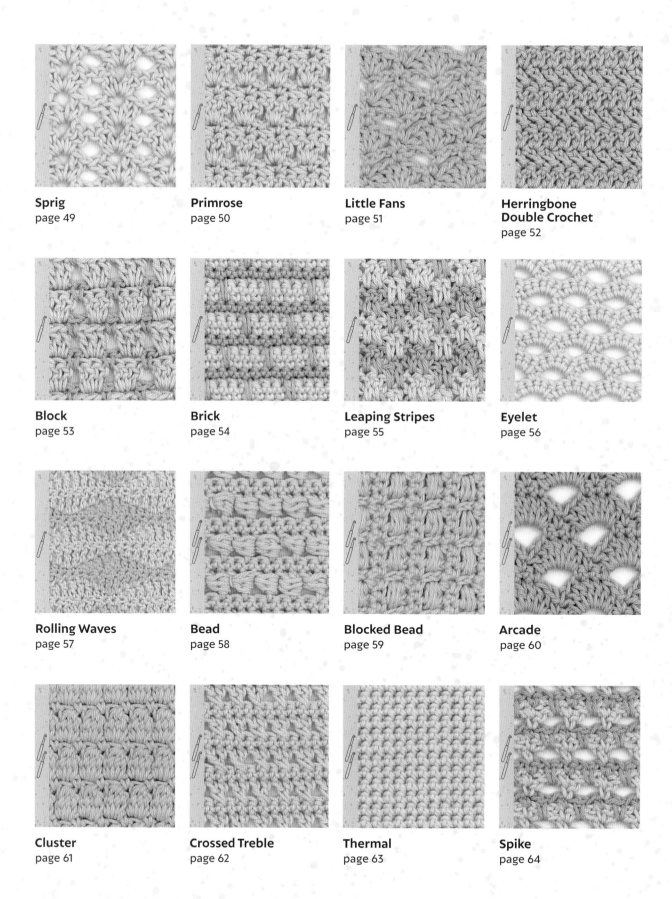

Sprig
page 49

Primrose
page 50

Little Fans
page 51

Herringbone Double Crochet
page 52

Block
page 53

Brick
page 54

Leaping Stripes
page 55

Eyelet
page 56

Rolling Waves
page 57

Bead
page 58

Blocked Bead
page 59

Arcade
page 60

Cluster
page 61

Crossed Treble
page 62

Thermal
page 63

Spike
page 64

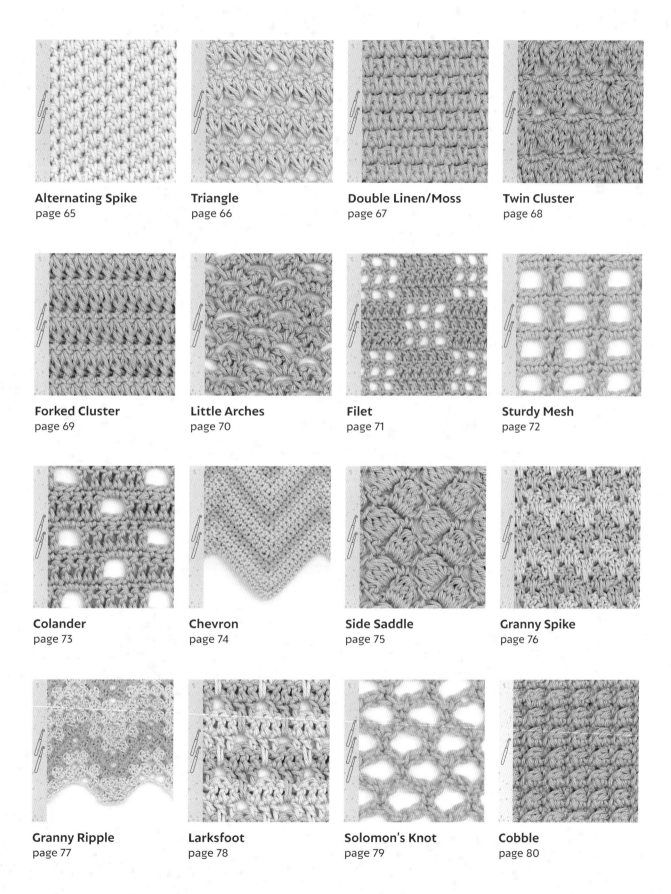

Alternating Spike
page 65

Triangle
page 66

Double Linen/Moss
page 67

Twin Cluster
page 68

Forked Cluster
page 69

Little Arches
page 70

Filet
page 71

Sturdy Mesh
page 72

Colander
page 73

Chevron
page 74

Side Saddle
page 75

Granny Spike
page 76

Granny Ripple
page 77

Larksfoot
page 78

Solomon's Knot
page 79

Cobble
page 80

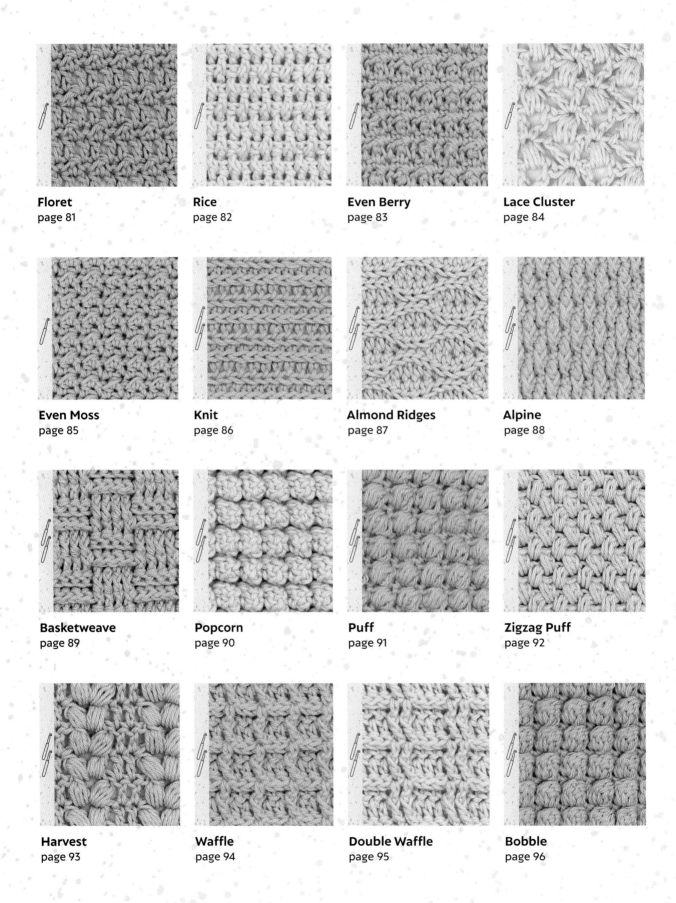

Floret
page 81

Rice
page 82

Even Berry
page 83

Lace Cluster
page 84

Even Moss
page 85

Knit
page 86

Almond Ridges
page 87

Alpine
page 88

Basketweave
page 89

Popcorn
page 90

Puff
page 91

Zigzag Puff
page 92

Harvest
page 93

Waffle
page 94

Double Waffle
page 95

Bobble
page 96

Feather
page 97

Corded Ridge
page 98

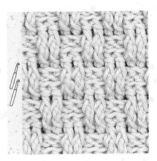

Mini Basketweave
page 99

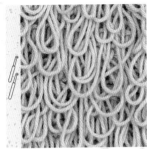

Loop
page 100

Diamond Waffle
page 101

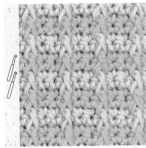

Bar
page 102

Royal Ridge
page 103

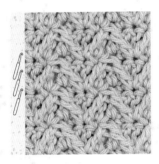

Arrow
page 104

Crocodile
page 105

Celtic Weave
page 106

Jasmine
page 107

Single-colour Granny Square
page 110

Multi-coloured Granny Square
page 112

Solid Granny Square
page 114

Granny Triangle
page 116

Solid Granny Triangle
page 117

**Super Solid
Granny Square**
page 118

Filet Square
page 120

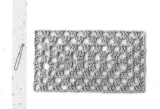

Granny Rectangle
page 122

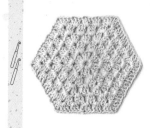

Granny Hexagon
page 124

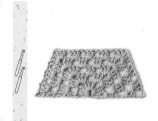

**Half Granny Hexagon –
horizontal**
page 126

**Half Granny Hexagon –
vertical**
page 127

Solid Hexagon
page 128

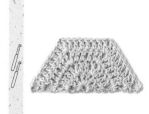

**Solid Half Hexagon –
horizontal**
page 130

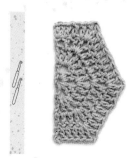

**Solid Half Hexagon –
vertical**
page 131

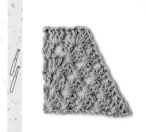

**Granny Hexagon –
quarter**
page 132

**Solid Hexagon –
quarter**
page 133

**Corner-to-Corner (C2C)
Granny Square**
page 134

**Corner-to-Corner (C2C)
Granny Rectangle**
page 136

V-Stitch Square
page 138

Circle in a Square
page 140

Bobble Circle Square
page 142

Block Stitch Square
page 144

Flower Hexagon
page 146

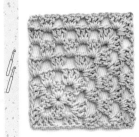

Mitred Granny Square
page 148

Solid Mitred Granny Square
page 150

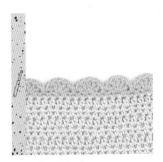

Shell
page 153

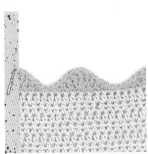

Wavy
page 154

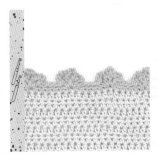

Triple Picot
page 155

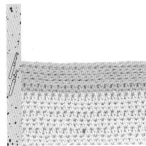

Camel
page 156

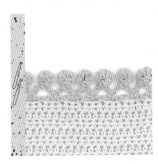

Pompom
page 157

PROJECTS 158

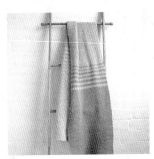

Faded Wrap
page 159

Fia Tote
page 162

Florence Blanket
page 166

INTRODUCTION

Hello and welcome to my stitch library. My name is Sarah-Jayne and I have been helping people learn to crochet since 2014.

I wrote my first book, *You Can Crochet with Bella Coco* in 2022, and I'm thrilled to be bringing you this brand-new book full of my favourite stitches.

While my first book is designed for absolute beginners, this book will take you further on your crochet journey. Explore new stitches, discover new techniques, and gain a deeper knowledge of the art of crochet so that you can really explore your own crochet style. I'm also delighted to include both US and UK terms throughout the library, so that you can enjoy crocheting your new favourite patterns wherever you are in the world.

Have fun crocheting!

Sarah-Jayne Fragola

EQUIPMENT & TOOLS

1 Crochet hook

These come in a variety of materials such as metal, plastic, wood and bamboo, and the heads are either inline or tapered. You can find crochet hooks from as small as 0.6mm (US 14) to as big as 30mm (T/X). While the metric system of measuring crochet hooks is popular, different countries and manufacturers also use alternative number or letter systems. See the conversion chart on the front cover flap for the most common sizes.

2 Yarn needles

These are needles with large eyes, and they are perfect for weaving in ends and sewing seams. They can be made of metal or plastic and have a straight or bent tip.

3 Cutting tools

Sharp embroidery scissors, snips or yarn cutters are needed when changing colours or fastening off rows.

4 Stitch markers

Used to mark the beginning or end of rows/rounds, or marking key stitches, markers come in a variety of shapes, sizes and colours, as well as different clasps.

5 Fabric clips

Clips come in handy when sewing different pieces together, as they can hold lots of layers in place while working.

6 Measuring tools

Fabric and plastic measuring tapes can be easily transported; hard rulers are great for checking gauge/tension.

7 Pins

Pins are great for holding work in place and also when blocking work. You can use single pins or larger blocking pins that have multiple pins attached. If you are using pins for blocking, just make sure that they are the kind that are rust free!

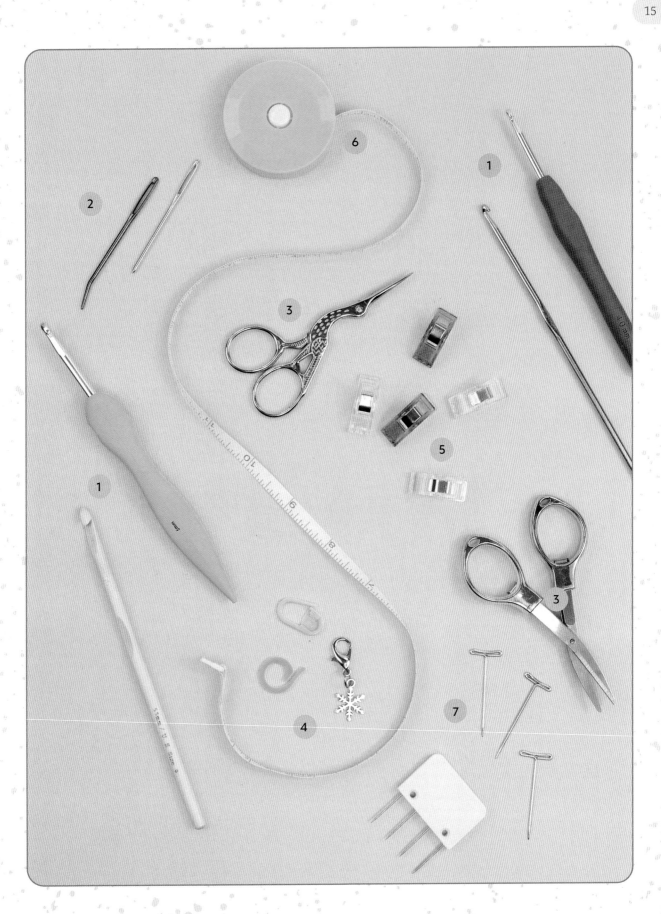

YARNS & FIBRES

YARN FORMS

Yarn can be purchased in many forms; here are the most common.

1 Skeins

Also sometimes known as a bullet skein, a skein can be pulled from the outside or the centre. Check the yarn label for instructions.

2 Hanks

When a yarn had been hand-dyed, it is usually presented in a hank. This type of yarn will need to be unravelled then wound before it's used. To unravel the yarn, you can drape the hank over a chair or round a yarn swift; you can then wind it into a ball by hand or use a yarn-ball winder to wind the hank into a cake.

3 Balls (not shown)

These are usually rewound from a skein or hank of yarn. It's important that you do not wind the yarn too tightly as this may affect the fibres. This is a good way to wind left-over or scrap yarn.

4 Cakes

These are made using a yarn-ball winder, often after being rewound from a skein or a hank. Cakes can can be much easier to work from. Being flat on the top and bottom, they don't roll around; you can also easily pull yarn from the centre of the cake. Once you have used half of the cake, turn it on its side, which will make it easier crochet with.

5 Cones

The yarn is wound around a plastic or sturdy cardboard cone. Cones usually contain a larger amount of yarn then a regular skein.

6 Donuts

These are similar to cakes as you pull the yarn from the centre, meaning you may not need to rewind them into balls. Many luxury yarns like Merino and cashmere are presented this way.

YARN TYPES

Yarn can be made from many different fibres. These can be natural fibres or synthetic fibres. Each will have their own unique characteristics and will be more suited to some projects than others. Whichever you use often comes down to personal preference, cultural belief or the type of project you are working on.

Natural fibres: These come from plants or animal hair. This includes wool (sheep), cashmere (goat), alpaca, mohair (Angora goat), linen, bamboo and silk.

Synthetic fibres: These are man-made fibres, such as acrylic, polyester or nylon.

YARN WEIGHTS

Below, you will find a table listing different yarn weights. As with many things in crochet, different terms are used in different countries, and each country uses a particular system to categorize yarn weight.

0 weight (lace).

1 weight (super fine).

2 weight (fine).

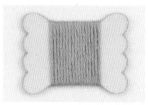

3 weight (light).

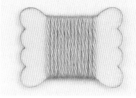

4 weight (medium).

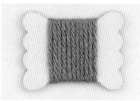

5 weight (bulky).

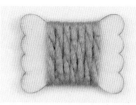

6 weight (super bulky).

7 weight (jumbo).

SYMBOL	CATEGORY	UK NAME	US NAME	AUSTRALIAN NAME
0	lace	1-ply	laceweight	2-ply
1	super fine	2-ply	baby/fingering/sock	3-ply
2	fine	3-ply	baby/sport	5-ply
3	light	DK/4-ply	light worsted	8-ply
4	medium	aran	worsted	10-ply
5	bulky	chunky/craft/rug	bulky	12-ply
6	super bulky	super chunky	super bulky	14-ply
7	jumbo	ultra, roving	jumbo	16-ply

GAUGE

Crochet gauge (also known as tension) comes into play on
many occasions. There are many things that can affect your gauge,
such as the type of yarn or hook you're using, the way you hold your
hook or yarn, how you have prepared your yarn, and your positioning.
A lot of 'newbie' crocheters tend to have fairly tight gauge,
which makes it harder to work into the stitches. But, after practice,
you soon get a feel for what's right, and find your own rhythm.

HOW DO I MEASURE GAUGE?

If you are working from a pattern, usually it will tell
you how many stitches and how many rows should
sit within a certain area of your main crochet stitch
pattern (usually within a 4in/10cm square). Before
you make a start on the pattern, it's a good idea to
crochet a swatch so you can test your own gauge
against the designer's. It's especially important to do
this when making garments; after all, nobody wants
to spend hours making a sweater only to find it
doesn't fit how it should!

You will need to crochet a swatch that is bigger than
the dimensions of the gauge stated in the pattern.
This is so that you can accurately measure the
stitches within the main body of the swatch.

I recommend using a hard ruler to measure gauge:
I find fabric and plastic tape measures can stretch
over time.

Measuring stitches: Place the ruler horizontally over
the work with the starting point at the beginning of
a stitch. Across one row, count how many stitches
are within the specified measurement (including
the spaces between stitches), making sure you are
counting to the end of the last stitch.

Measuring rows: First establish the base of a row
and the top of a row, remembering that part of
the stitch may be covered by the legs of the row
above. Place your ruler vertically over the work,
with the starting point at the base of a row. Count
upwards how many rows are within the specified
measurement, making sure to finish at the top of
the top row.

I HAVE MY MEASUREMENTS, NOW WHAT?

If your stitches and rows match what is stated in the pattern... congratulations, you've 'hit gauge'! If not, don't worry: there are a few things you can do to correct your personal gauge to match the pattern designer's.

Correcting stitches

If you have too few or too many stitches, it might be a case of simply changing your hook size. If you have too many stitches, try going a up half or full hook size. If you don't have enough stitches, try going down a half or full hook size. Repeat this until you hit the right gauge.

Correcting rows

Changing to a different hook size may help with your stitches; however, there may be occasions when the number of stitches are correct but your rows are off.

In this case... say hello to the golden loop!

The golden loop (first brought to us by the late Jean Leinhauser) is something that I wish I'd known about much sooner in my crochet journey. Having an awareness of this can really change how you look at your own crochet work, and help you to adapt accordingly. The golden loop relates to the loop on the hook after you've pulled the working yarn through a stitch. It's this loop that will determine the height of your stitch and, ultimately, will affect your row height.

When thinking about the golden loop, it's important to know what kind of crocheter you are. In my experience there are three types: Yankers, Riders and Lifters.

Yankers: The golden loop is pulled downwards; this is usually because the crocheter either 'yanks' on the yarn and/or the hook is held with the head pointing downwards. This produces a shorter stitch.

Riders: Considered the middle of the road; this crocheter has an even gauge and/or holds the hook horizontally.

Lifters: Here, the golden loops are 'lifted' upwards; this is because the crocheter has loose gauge and/or they hold their hook with the head pointing upwards. This produces a taller stitch.

I recommend you make a small swatch and pay attention to what category you may fall into. Once you establish your own personal gauge style, you can use this to hit the desired gauge for the pattern.

If you have too many rows, adjust the golden loop to make it tighter; this will reduce the row height (for example, you may be a Lifter, but the designer is a Rider).

If you don't have enough rows, adjust the golden loop to make it looser which will increase the row height (for example, you may be a Yanker, but the designer is a Lifter).

The golden loop.

Yankers (pulling on yarn).

Riders (even tension).

Lifters (drawing up tall loops on the hook).

BASIC TECHNIQUES

All the key know-how you'll need to help you when you start to create your stitches, shapes and borders can be found in this section. Each technique contains step-by-step instructions with corresponding images.

If you need to remind yourself of how to work the basic stitches, please see the instructions under the relevant stitch in the 'Abbreviations' section on pages 171–175.

SLIP KNOT

A slip knot is one of the most basic techniques you need to know.
We need to create a slip knot so that we can start to build our foundation chain.

  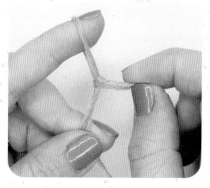

1 From front to back, loop the tail end of the yarn around your index finger. Hold the working end of the yarn between your thumb and middle finger, then cross the tail end of the yarn in front of it.

2 Loop the working yarn over your index finger, from front to back.

3 Lift the back loop over the front loop and release it from your finger. This creates the slip knot, which you can then transfer to your crochet hook. Once the loop is on your hook, tighten the loop up against your crochet hook by pulling on the working yarn.

MAKING A CHAIN

A chain usually forms the foundation of a project, which is why it is often referred to as a 'foundation' or 'starting chain'. Chaining is also used at the beginning of a row, to make what is known as a 'turning chain'. A turning chain ensures you're working at the right height to make the next stitch.

Foundation chain too tight?

Try going up a hook size when making your foundation chain, then switch to the size of hook recommended in the pattern when working the rest of the rows or rounds.

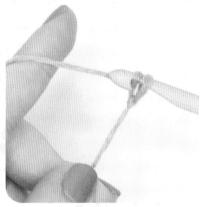

1 With the slip knot already slipped on to your hook, bring your hook under and around the yarn – this is know as 'yarn over' (yo) or 'yarn round hook' (yrh).

2 Pull the yarn through the loop on the hook.

3 One chain made. Simply keep repeating steps 1 and 2 until you have the number of chains instructed in the pattern.

WORKING INTO A CHAIN

There are two common ways of working into chains. Typically, you will work into the top/left-hand/back loop of a chain only (see the left-hand image), ignoring the 'back bump/spine' behind it. However, once you become more confident, working into this back bump/spine instead (see the right-hand image) will create a neater finish and you have the option to work into the front and back loops of the stitch too (handy when crocheting clothing or adding a border to your work).

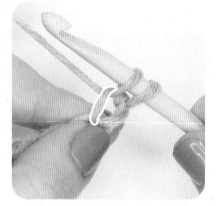

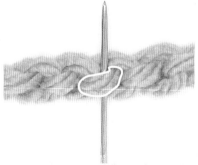

WORKING INTO STITCHES

You'll have noticed that, once a stitch is made, it makes two loops on the top edge of a row. These are called 'top loops'. These two loops have a braided appearance, and look like a sideways 'V'. The yarn needle inserted in the crochet shown to the right, in the top two images, indicates these top loops.

To work into stitches, simply pass the hook under both these loops.

Side view of top loops. *Bird's-eye view of top loops.*

Inserting a hook into the top loops.

WORKING INTO A CHAIN SPACE

This is a method usually used in granny squares or to create lace-like holes in your crochet. Instead of inserting the hook into a stitch, insert it into the space made by crocheting one or more chains in the previous row or round.

Here, I'm making a granny square, and have just worked three double crochet (*UK treble crochet*) stitches into a chain space (see the circled area).

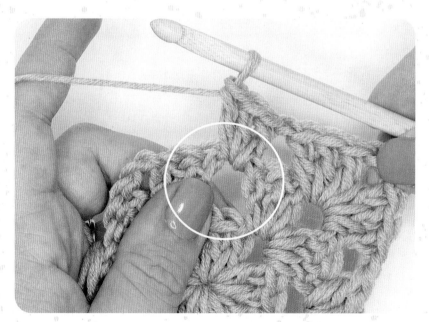

Chain space, with three double crochet (UK treble crochet) stitches worked into it.

WORKING IN THE ROUND: CHAIN METHODS

To make circular-shaped projects, or to make granny squares, you will often need to work in the round. There are different ways of 'working in the round', each giving you different results. The foundation-ring method is used for projects where you want to make tubular shapes. The flat-circle method is useful for flatter circular shapes (like granny squares). For a more advanced method of making a flat circle, which has no gap in the middle, you could use the magic ring (adjustable loop) method instead, which you can find on page 26.

Foundation-ring method

This is the easiest method, and is sometimes known as the foundation-chain method. By joining the first and last stitch of a foundation chain, you can form this foundation ring.

1 Start by making the required number of chains for your foundation chain. Slip stitch into the first chain.

2 Crochet your turning chain then work your stitches into each chain to complete one round.

3 Slip stitch into the first stitch of the round. Repeat steps 2 and 3 as necessary.

Flat-circle method

This method consists of making a few chains and then working your stitches into the first chain to make a ring. If you don't like making a magic ring (adjustable loop), this is the next best thing! I'm working single crochet (*UK double crochet*) stitches here.

1 Start by making the required number of chains.

2 Insert your hook into the first chain and work your first stitch. Continue to work all the remaining stitches into the same first chain, a shown.

3 Insert the hook into the first stitch then slip stitch to join the ends of the round.

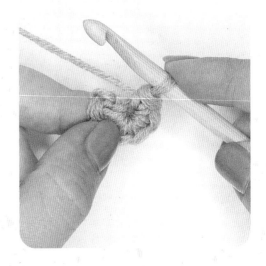

WORKING IN THE ROUND: MAGIC RING

This method, also known as the 'magic circle' or 'adjustable loop', is used to create a tight circle when working in the round. It is ideal for projects like amigurumi as it doesn't leave a little hole in the middle of your circle.

There are different ways of starting a magic ring; the steps below show the one-finger method.

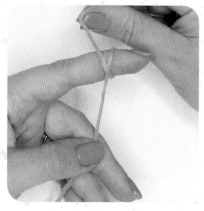

1 Holding on to the tail end of your ball of yarn, wrap the yarn over and around your index finger to create an 'X'.

2 Bring the working (ball) end of your yarn down to meet the tail end and hold in place with your thumb and middle finger.

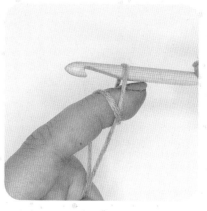

3 Insert the hook under the loop closest to the fingertip.

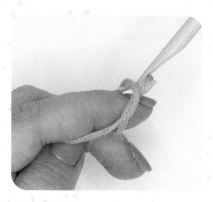

4 Grab the next loop then pull this under the first loop.

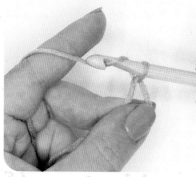

5 Yarn over ('yo' or 'yrh').

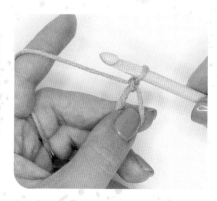

6 Pull through the loop to make a chain. At this point, you can chain the number needed to create the height for the specific stitch you are working. I will chain 3 as I am working double crochet (*UK treble crochet*) stitch.

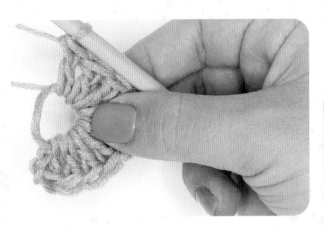 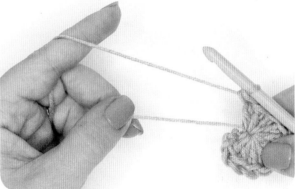

7 Work your stitches into the magic ring (adjustable loop) while also working over the tail end. To do this, simply treat the inside of the ring as a stitch, and as a row of crochet if you're working multiple stitches.

8 Pull the tail end tight to close the circle. Depending on your pattern, you'll now have two options: you can begin the next round by crocheting into the first stitch immediately, or you can join the ends of your magic ring (adjustable loop) by joining the last stitch to the starting chain or first stitch with slip stitch.

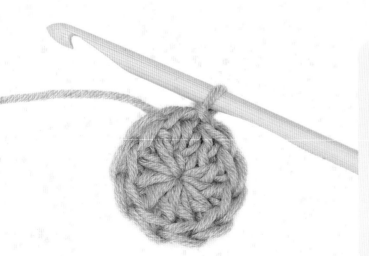

Tip

You may need to adjust the size of the ring at step 6, depending on how many stitches you will work in step 7 and how tall they are. To make the ring smaller, gently pull on the tail end of the yarn. If you wish to make the ring bigger, gently pull on the right-hand side of the ring (if you are left-handed, this will be the left side).

FASTENING OFF

Whether it is to change colour or simply to end your project, at some point you will have to fasten off (or 'tie off') your yarn. Below, I'll show you the simplest way to do it. This process is the same, regardless of whatever stitch you use.

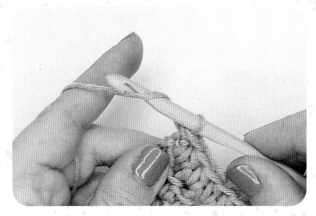

1 After working your last st, create a single chain: yarn over ('yo' or 'yrh') and pull through the loop on the hook.

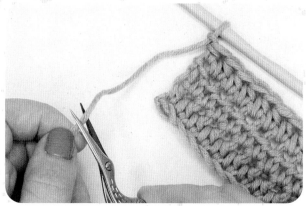

2 Snip the yarn, leaving a 4–6in (10–15cm) tail.

3 Pull on your hook to draw the tail end out of the loop.

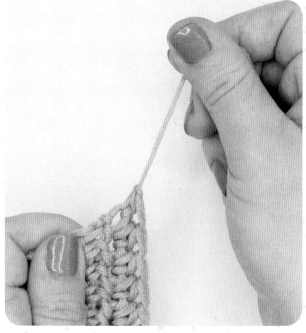

4 Pull on the tail end to secure it.

WEAVING IN LOOSE ENDS

Once you have fastened off your yarn, you will need to deal with those tail ends. Doing this effectively will be important for the longevity of your project. I use the 'rule of three', which simply means you are going to do three 'passes', working back and forth across the rows.

1 Thread the tail end on to a yarn needle. Weave in and out of the fibres on the wrong side of the work for around 2in (5cm). This is your first 'pass'.

2 Working in the opposite direction, weave the needle in and out of the fibres following a slightly different path to your first pass. This is your second pass.

3 Working in the opposite direction once more, weave your needle in and out of the fibres. This is your third pass.

4 Snip off the remaining tail end to complete.

INVISIBLE JOIN

This technique helps create a tidy join in a circular project, as it doesn't leave a visible bump where you fasten off your yarn. This method is also used to join the end and beginning stitches when working in a circle or around a piece.

Tip

If the stitch count isn't important (for example, because you're on the final row of your project), you can place the needle through the first stitch of the round in step 1. Otherwise, always skip the first stitch and insert the needle into the second to avoid adding an extra stitch.

1 Thread the yarn end onto a yarn needle and insert it through the top of the second stitch in the round, from the right side (RS) to wrong side (WS).

2 Pull the yarn through, being careful not to pull too tight.

3 Insert the yarn needle through the back loop only of the last stitch of the round from the right side (RS) to the wrong side (WS).

4 Pull the yarn through and adjust the gauge so that the stitch is the same as the other stitches. Weave the loose end into the wrong side (WS) of your work.

Finishing your work in this way means that the final stitch is indistinguishable from the rest.

COLOUR CHANGES

For many projects, you will need to change to a different-coloured yarn. Here's how to do it.

You can change colour at the end of the row, or at any point during a row. I will demonstrate using single crochet (*UK double crochet*); however, this technique can be used with any stitch. Simply perform the technique on the last step of a stitch.

1 Work the necessary stitches in the first colour until the last 'pull through'.

2 Drop your first colour then catch the new colour with the hook, making sure you leave a 4in (10cm) tail of your new colour for weaving in later.

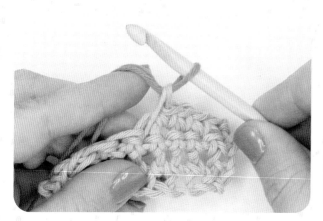

3 Pull through the new colour.

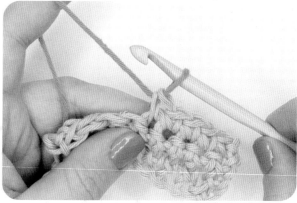

4 Gently tug the tail end of your first colour to prevent the loops from getting bigger, and then continue to crochet in the new colour.

ANATOMY OF A STITCH

Having a good understanding of the anatomy of a crochet stitch will be
a huge benefit when exploring more advanced stitch combinations later,
where you may need to work into different parts of a stitch to create a certain
look or texture. Refer back to these pages if you need to remind yourself where
to insert your hook for a particular stitch.

ANATOMY OF A CHAIN

A chain is formed of three loops: the front loop, the back loop
and the back bump.

When you look at your chain from the top you will see a series
of interlocking V's. Each V is a chain, and from this angle you
can see the front loop and the back loop. The back loop is the
farthest away you and the loop that you will typically work
into as a beginner crocheter. The front loop is the loop closest
to you.

If you flip your chain over, you will see the back bumps;
the bump is sometimes known as the 'spine' of the stitch
(see also the opposite page for more information and a
photograph). Each V on the front of the chain will have a
corresponding back bump.

Back loop.

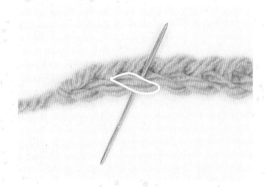

Front loop.

FRONT LOOPS AND BACK LOOPS

When a stitch is made, it will create another series of interlocking V's at the top of the stitch. These are called the 'top loops' (which you encountered earlier on page 24).

In a lot of instances, you will work through both of these loops to make a stitch; however, stitches may require you to work into just one of these loops.

The front loop is the loop closest to you and the back loop is the loop farthest away from you. Working into the front loops only (FLO) or the back loops only (BLO) creates texture as it tilts the top of a stitch, forming a ridge.

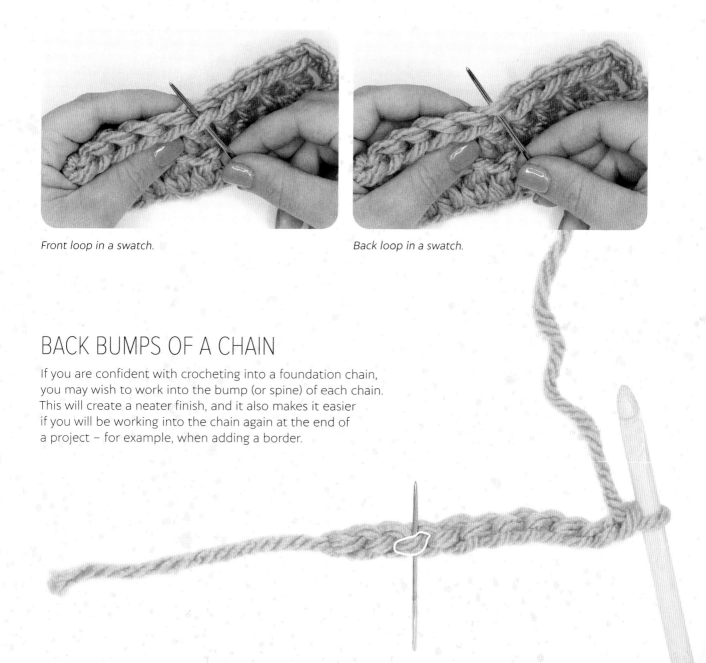

Front loop in a swatch.

Back loop in a swatch.

BACK BUMPS OF A CHAIN

If you are confident with crocheting into a foundation chain, you may wish to work into the bump (or spine) of each chain. This will create a neater finish, and it also makes it easier if you will be working into the chain again at the end of a project – for example, when adding a border.

STITCH POSTS

The post of a stitch is the main body of a stitch. It can be very tall, depending on the stitch itself. You will work around the post of the stitch when making a front post (FP) or a back post (BP) stitch. Working around a stitch post creates a raised effect, and is often used to create cable-like textures in crochet.

STITCH LEGS

These are located at the base of the stitch, and it's where it connects to the row below. For some stitches, you insert the hook in the small gap between the legs; this makes the row of stitches shorter in height, but you're left with a denser crochet fabric.

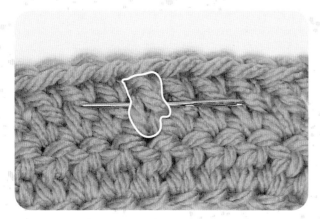

THIRD LOOPS

When working half double crochet (*UK half treble*), the yarn over before you insert the hook into the next stitch creates an extra diagonal loop on the front and back of the stitch. This is called a third loop.

When you work into third loops, they will push the top loops of the stitch to the side facing away from you, creating a beautiful textured 'stripe' of stitches.

The third loop (white) on the right side, and the front loop of the stitch to which it's connected (blue).

The third loop (white) on the wrong side, and the top loops of the stitch to which it's connected (blue).

BLOCKING

I will share a few different blocking methods with you in a moment, but the basic principle of blocking is to ensure that your work forms a particular shape or size, and to help with stitch placement – particularly useful if your work features lace-like patterns.

Do you need to block everything? Honestly, not really, and it depends on the project. Always check your pattern notes to see what is suggested. Often you won't need to block larger items like a blanket, but generally you will find projects such as garments and granny squares require blocking to achieve a certain size or shape.

Before blocking.

After blocking.

Spray blocking

This method is great for small items such as granny squares.

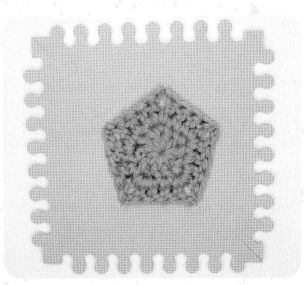

1 Using a spray bottle, spritz the work to make it damp but not soaking.

2 Place the work on to a blocking mat and pin into place with rust-proof pins.

3 Check the sizing, as per the pattern instructions or your own preference, and adjust the pins as necessary.

4 Leave the item to dry completely, then remove the pins.

Tip

Instead of a blocking mat (shown above and left) you can also use blocking boards, which work in a similar way. These are flat boards with evenly spaced holes. The work is attached using wooden dowels, which hold it in place.

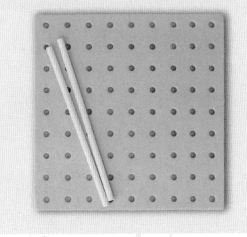

Soak blocking

This works well with natural fibres, large items and more complex projects such as garments.

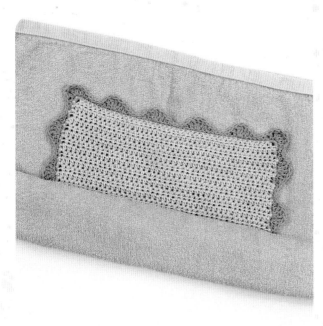

1 Submerge the item into water containing wool wash. Once the item has soaked up as much water as it can, carefully squeeze (don't wring) out excess water, taking care not to pull on the fibres.

2 Lay the item on to a towel and slowly start to roll, pressing the towel as you do this to remove more water from the item inside.

3 Place the item on to a blocking mat (or even a few clean, folded towels) and pin into place with rust-proof pins.

4 Check the sizing, as per the pattern instructions or your own preference, and adjust the pins as necessary.

5 Leave the item to dry completely, then remove the pins.

Steam blocking

You can steam block using an iron or a garment steamer and a blocking mat. A garment steamer is generally better as you'll have more control. If you do opt for using an iron, be careful not to touch your work with the iron itself. I recommend a garment steamer if you're steaming acrylic yarn, as under the iron your project could melt!

Once you have steamed the item, it will be damp. Although you may have seen a change in shape from the heat alone, you will still need to pin it out on a blocking mat, blocking board or towel, and allow to dry fully.

STITCHES

In this section of the book you will find the stitch library. The first part covers the basic crochet stitches; the second part combines these stitches (plus a few special ones) to create simple stitch combinations; and the third part finishes off the section with some stunning textured stitches.

The information about each stitch will be given alongside a photograph of a swatch made up in that specific stitch's pattern, which you can adapt for your own projects. Throughout the stitch library, both US and UK terms are given – with US first, and the UK term following in italics and inside round brackets.

WHAT YOU'LL FIND FOR EACH STITCH

Skill level: This will state whether the stitch is classed as beginner, intermediate or advanced. Please note that this is just a guide – I'd always encourage you to give it a go!

Multiples: A repeat or multiple will be important when starting your project or combining different stitches. It's a formula that ensures you can always recreate your chosen pattern across any width and height. The multiple will often follow with a '+' and another number. This additional number is for the turning chain, plus any extra chains required to complete the stitch pattern repeat. For example, if the stitch is a '3 + 2', this means you will chain 3 stitches at a time for your foundation row to get to your desired width then add an additional 2 stitches at the very end.

Stitches used: A list of stitches that are used within the overall stitch pattern. Refer to the 'Abbreviations' section on pages 171–175, too, if you need to. There may be some additional information about any special stitches used.

Pattern notes: These give you important information to help you create the stitch.

Instructions: These detail how to start, work the repeat and finish the stitch pattern, written in crochet shorthand. Unless stated, there is no wrong or right side to the patterns.

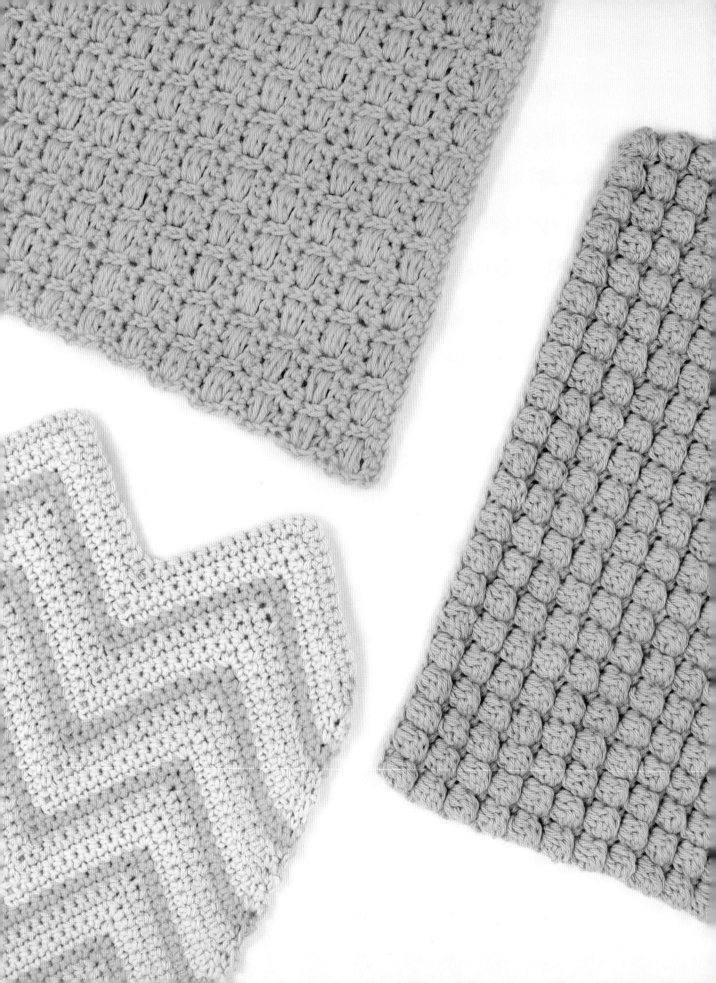

IMPORTANT NOTE

For this Basic Stitches section, on pages 40–43, we'll cover the formula for making each of the five basic crochet stitches into a larger piece of crochet fabric.

If you need to remind yourself how to work each actual stitch, please refer to the 'Abbreviations' section on pages 171–175.

Single Crochet
UK DOUBLE CROCHET

Skill level
Beginner

Multiples
1 + 1

Stitch used
sc (*UK dc*)

Colour
Stormy Grey

INSTRUCTIONS

Row 1: sc (*UK dc*) in second ch from hook (skipped ch does not count as st), sc (*UK dc*) in each ch across. Turn.

Row 2: 1 ch (does not count as a st here and throughout), sc (*UK dc*) in each st across. Turn.

Rep Row 2 until desired height.

Fasten off and sew in ends.

Half Double Crochet
UK HALF TREBLE CROCHET

Skill level
Beginner

Multiples
1 + 2

Stitch used
hdc (*UK htr*)

Colour
Sea foam

INSTRUCTIONS

Row 1: hdc (*UK htr*) in third ch from hook (skipped 2-ch count as st), hdc (*UK htr*) in each ch across. Turn.

Row 2: 2 ch (counts as st here and throughout), hdc (*UK htr*) in each st across. Turn.

Rep Row 2 until desired height.

Fasten off and sew in ends.

Double Crochet
UK TREBLE CROCHET

Skill level
Beginner

Multiples
1 + 3

Stitch used
dc (*UK tr*)

Colour
Blush Pink

INSTRUCTIONS

Row 1: dc (*UK tr*) in fourth ch from hook (skipped 3-ch counts as st), dc (*UK tr*) in each ch across. Turn.

Row 2: 3 ch (counts as st here and throughout), dc (*UK tr*) in each st across. Turn.

Rep Row 2 until desired height.

Fasten off and sew in ends.

Treble Crochet
UK DOUBLE TREBLE CROCHET

Skill level
Beginner

Multiples
1 + 4

Stitch used
tr (*UK dtr*)

Colour
Vanilla Cream

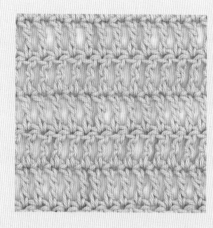

INSTRUCTIONS

Row 1: tr (*UK dtr*) in fifth ch from hook (skipped 4-ch counts as st), tr (*UK dtr*) in each ch across. Turn.

Row 2: 4 ch (counts as st here and throughout), tr (*UK dtr*) in each st across. Turn.

Rep Row 2 until desired height.

Fasten off and sew in ends.

Double Treble Crochet
UK TRIPLE TREBLE CROCHET

Skill level
Beginner

Multiples
1 + 5

Stitch used
dtr (*UK trtr*)

Colour
Stormy Grey

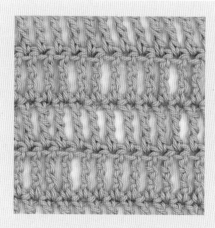

INSTRUCTIONS

Row 1: dtr (*UK trtr*) in sixth ch from hook (skipped 5-ch count as st), dtr (*UK trtr*) in each ch across. Turn.

Row 2: 5 ch (counts as st here and throughout), dtr (*UK trtr*) in each st across. Turn.

Rep Row 2 until desired height.

Fasten off and sew in ends.

Linen/moss

Skill level
Beginner

Multiples
2 + 1

Stitches used
ch, sc (*UK dc*)

Colour
Sea Foam

INSTRUCTIONS

Row 1: sc (*UK dc*) in third ch from hook (skipped 2-ch counts as sc (*UK dc*) and 1 ch), *1 ch, skip 1 ch, sc (*UK dc*) in next ch, rep from * across. Turn.

Row 2: 2 ch (counts as sc (*UK dc*) and 1 ch here and throughout), *sc (*UK dc*) in next ch sp, 1 ch, skip 1 sc (*UK dc*), rep from * across to 2-ch rem, sc (*UK dc*) in second of 2-ch. Turn.

Rep Row 2 until desired height.

Fasten off and sew in ends.

Suzette

Skill level
Beginner

Multiples
2 + 2

Stitches used
ch, sc (*UK dc*), dc (*UK tr*)

Colour
Pistachio Green

INSTRUCTIONS

Row 1: [sc (*UK dc*), dc (*UK tr*)] in second ch from hook (skipped ch does not count as st), skip next ch, *[sc (*UK dc*), dc (*UK tr*)] in next ch, skip next ch, rep from * until 1 ch rem, sc (*UK dc*) in last ch. Turn.

Row 2: 1 ch (does not count as st here or throughout), *[sc (*UK dc*), dc (*UK tr*)] in next sc (*UK dc*), skip 1 dc (*UK tr*), rep from * until 1 st rem, sc (*UK dc*) in last st. Turn.

Rep Row 2 until desired height.

Fasten off and sew in ends.

Houndstooth

Skill level
Beginner

Multiples
2 + 1

Stitches used
ch, sc (*UK dc*), dc (*UK tr*)

Colours
Vanilla cream (A),
Blush Pink (B)

INSTRUCTIONS

Row 1: sc (*UK dc*) in second ch from hook (skipped ch does not count as st), dc (*UK tr*) in next ch, [sc (*UK dc*) in next ch, dc (*UK tr*) in next ch] across, changing to yarn B in last yo of the last ch. Turn.

Row 2: 1 ch (does not count as st here or throughout), [sc (*UK dc*) in next st, dc (*UK tr*) in next st] across, changing to yarn A in last yo of the last st. Turn.

Rep Row 2, alternating between yarn A and B by changing colours in the last yo of the final st on each row, until desired height.

Fasten off and sew in ends.

Spider

Skill level
Beginner

Multiples
2 + 2

Stitches used
ch, sc (*UK dc*)

Colour
Pistachio Green

INSTRUCTIONS

Row 1: [sc (*UK dc*), 1 ch, sc (*UK dc*)] in second ch from hook (skipped ch does not count as st), *skip 1 ch, [sc (*UK dc*), 1 ch, sc (*UK dc*)] in same ch, rep from * across. Turn.

Row 2: *[sc (*UK dc*), 1 ch, sc (*UK dc*)] in next ch sp from previous row, rep from * across. Turn.

Rep Row 2 until desired height.

Fasten off and sew in ends.

Ripple

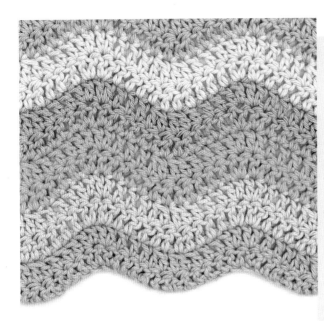

Skill level
Beginner

Multiples
12 + 3

Stitches used
ch, dc (*UK tr*)

Pattern note
For different effects with this stitch, you can change colours every one, two, three or more rows. If you wish to change colour for the next row, do so in the last yarn over of the last stitch.

Colours
Pistachio Green (A), Vanilla Cream (B), Blush Pink (C), Stormy Grey (D), Sea Foam (E)

INSTRUCTIONS

Row 1: with yarn A dc (*UK tr*) into fourth ch from hook (skipped 3-ch counts as dc (*UK tr*)), *dc (*UK tr*) in each of next 3 ch, [dc2tog (*UK tr2tog*) over next 2 ch] twice, dc (*UK tr*) into each of next 3 ch, **[work 2 dc (*UK 2 tr*) into next ch] twice, rep from * across, ending last rep at **, work 2 dc (*UK 2 tr*) in last ch, changing to yarn B in last yo of last st. Turn.

Row 2: 3 ch (counts as dc (*UK tr*) here and throughout), dc (*UK tr*) in same st as 3-ch, *dc (*UK tr*) in each of next 3 sts, [dc2tog (*UK tr2tog*) over next 2 sts] twice, dc (*UK tr*) in each of next 3 sts, **[work 2 dc (*UK 2 tr*) into next st] twice, rep from * across, ending last rep at **, work 2 dc (*UK 2 tr*) in last st, changing to yarn C in last yo of last st. Turn.

Rep Row 2 until desired height, changing to the next colour in your chosen sequence in last yo of last st.
Fasten off and sew in ends.

Grit

Skill level
Beginner

Multiples
2 + 1

Stitches used
ch, sc (*UK dc*)

Colour
Sea Foam

INSTRUCTIONS

Row 1: sc (*UK dc*) in second ch from hook (skipped ch does not count as st), *skip next ch, 2 sc (*UK 2 dc*) in next ch, rep from * across until 1 ch rem, sc (*UK dc*) in last ch. Turn.

Row 2: 1 ch (does not count as st here and throughout), sc (*UK dc*) in first st, *skip next st, 2 sc (*UK 2 dc*) in next st, rep from * across until 1 st rem, sc (*UK dc*) in last st. Turn.

Rep Row 2 until desired height.

Fasten off and sew in ends.

Crunch

Skill level
Beginner

Multiples
2 + 2

Stitches used
ch, sl st, hdc (*UK htr*)

Colour
Pistachio Green

INSTRUCTIONS

Row 1: sl st in second ch from hook, *hdc (*UK htr*), sl st in next st, rep from * across. Turn.

Row 2: 2 ch (counts as hdc (*UK htr*)), *sl st in the top of the hdc (*UK htr*) from the previous row, hdc (*UK htr*) into the sl st from the previous row, rep from * across. Turn.

Row 3: 1 ch (does not count as st), sl st in first st, *hdc (*UK htr*) in next st, sl st in next st, rep from * across. Turn.

Rep Rows 2 and 3 until desired height.

Fasten off and sew in ends.

Granny Stripe

Skill level
Beginner

Multiples
3 + 2

Stitches used
ch, sc (*UK dc*), dc (*UK tr*)

Pattern note
For different effects with this stitch, you can change colours every one, two, three or more rows. If you wish to change colour for the next row, do so in the last yarn over of the last stitch.

Colours
Every row colour change:
Vanilla cream (A), Sea Foam (B), Blush Pink (C)

Every 2 rows colour change:
Stormy Grey (A), Vanilla Cream (B), Sea Foam (C)

Every 3 rows colour change:
Blush Pink (A), Pistachio Green (B), Vanilla Cream (C)

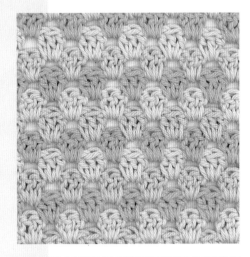
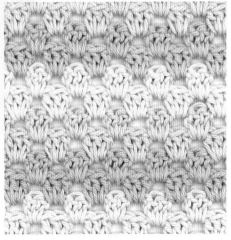
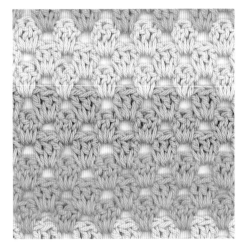

INSTRUCTIONS

Row 1: sc (*UK dc*) in second ch from hook and each ch across. Turn.

Row 2: 3 ch (counts as dc (*UK tr*) here and throughout), dc (*UK tr*) in same st as 3-ch, *skip 2 sts, 3 dc (*UK 3 tr*) in next st, rep from * until 3 sts rem, skip 2 sts, 2 dc (*UK 2 tr*) in last st. Turn.

Row 3: 3 ch, skip next st, *3 dc (*UK 3 tr*) in sp between clusters from previous row, skip 3 sts, rep from * until 3 sts rem, 3 dc (*UK 3 tr*) in sp between clusters, skip next st, dc (*UK tr*) in top of 3-ch. Turn.

Row 4: 3 ch, dc (*UK tr*) in sp between first and second st from previous row, *skip 3 sts, 3 dc (*UK 3 tr*) in sp between clusters from previous row, rep from * until 4 sts rem, skip 3 sts, dc (*UK tr*) in sp between last 2 sts, dc (*UK tr*) in top of 3-ch. Turn.

Rep Rows 3 and 4 until desired height.

Fasten off and sew in ends.

Wattle

Skill level
Beginner

Multiples
3 + 3

Stitches used
ch, sc (*UK dc*), dc (*UK tr*), hdc (*UK htr*)

Colour
Sea Foam

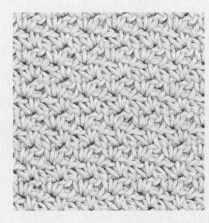

INSTRUCTIONS

Row 1: [sc (*UK dc*), 1 ch, dc (*UK tr*)] in third ch from hook (skipped 2-ch does not count as a st), skip 2 ch, *[sc (*UK dc*), 1 ch, dc (*UK tr*)] in next ch, skip 2 ch, rep from * until 1 ch rem, hdc (*UK htr*) in last ch. Turn.

Row 2: 1 ch (does not count as st here and throughout), skip hdc (*UK htr*) and dc (*UK tr*), [sc (*UK dc*), 1 ch, dc (*UK tr*)] in ch sp, *skip next 2 sts, [sc (*UK dc*), 1 ch, dc (*UK tr*)] in ch sp, rep from * until 1 st rem, hdc (*UK htr*) in last st. Turn.

Rep Row 2 until desired height.

Fasten off and sew in ends.

V Stitch

Skill level
Beginner

Multiples
3 + 3

Stitches used
ch, dc (*UK tr*)

Colour
Vanilla Cream

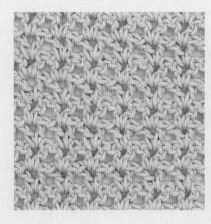

INSTRUCTIONS

Row 1: [dc (*UK tr*), 1 ch, dc (*UK tr*)] in fourth ch from hook (skipped 3-ch counts as dc (*UK tr*)), *skip 2 ch, [dc (*UK tr*), 1 ch, dc (*UK tr*)] in next ch, rep from * until 2 ch rem, skip 1 ch, dc (*UK tr*) in last ch. Turn.

Row 2: 3 ch (counts as dc (*UK tr*) here and throughout), [dc (*UK tr*), 1 ch, dc (*UK tr*)] in each 1-ch sp across, dc (*UK tr*) in top of 3-ch. Turn.

Rep Row 2 until desired height.

Fasten off and sew in ends.

Shell

Skill level
Beginner

Multiples
6 + 2

Stitches used
ch, sc (*UK dc*), ShSt –
see 'Special stitch' below,
dc (*UK tr*)

Special stitch
ShSt = Shell Stitch: work 5 dc
(*UK 5 tr*) into indicated stitch.

Colour
Stormy Grey

INSTRUCTIONS

Row 1: sc (*UK dc*) in second ch from hook (skipped ch does not count as st), *skip 2 ch, work a ShSt into next st, skip 2 ch, sc (*UK dc*), rep from * across. Turn.

Row 2: 1 ch (does not count as st here or throughout), 3 dc (*UK 3 tr*) in first st, *skip 2 sts, sc (*UK dc*) in middle dc (*UK tr*) of next ShSt, skip 2 sts, ShSt in the next sc (*UK dc*), rep from * across working 3 dc (*UK 3 tr*) in last sc (*UK dc*). Turn.

Row 3: 1 ch, sc (*UK dc*) in first st, *ShSt in next sc (*UK dc*), skip 2 sts, sc (*UK dc*) in middle dc (*UK tr*) of next ShSt, skip 2 sts, rep from * across working last sc (*UK dc*) in last st.

Rep Rows 2 and 3 until desired height.

Fasten off and sew in ends.

Sprig

Skill level
Beginner

Multiples
4 + 3

Stitches used
ch, dc (*UK tr*), sl st

Colour
Sea Foam

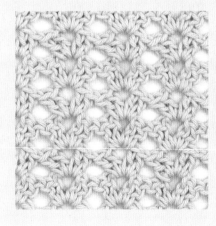

INSTRUCTIONS

Row 1: 2 dc (*UK 2 tr*) in fourth ch from hook (skipped 3-ch counts as dc (*UK tr*)), 2 ch, 2 dc (*UK 2 tr*) in next ch, *skip 2 ch, 2 dc (*UK 2 tr*) in next ch, 2 ch, 2 dc (*UK 2 tr*) in next ch, rep from * until 2 ch rem, skip 1 ch, dc (*UK tr*) in last ch. Turn.

Row 2: 3 ch (counts as dc (*UK tr*)), [2 dc (*UK 2 tr*), 2 ch, 2 dc (*UK 2 tr*)] in each ch sp across, dc (*UK tr*) into top of 3-ch. Turn.

Rep Row 2 until desired size.

Final Row: 3 ch, *sl st into next ch sp, 3 ch, rep from * across, sl st in top of 3-ch.

Fasten off and sew in ends.

Primrose

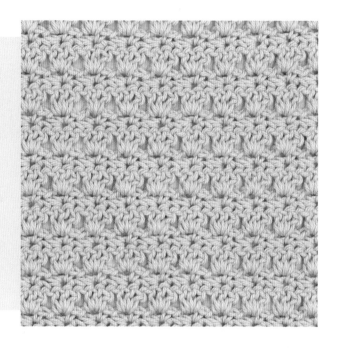

Skill level
Beginner

Multiples
3 + 2

Stitches used
ch, sc (*UK dc*), hdc (*UK htr*), dc (*UK tr*)

Colour
Vanilla Cream

INSTRUCTIONS

Row 1: [sc (*UK dc*), 2 ch, sc (*UK dc*)] in third ch from hook (skipped 2-ch counts as hdc (*UK htr*)), *skip 2 ch, [sc (*UK dc*), 2 ch, sc (*UK dc*)] in next ch, rep from * until 2 ch rem, skip 1 ch, hdc (*UK htr*) in last ch. Turn.

Row 2: 3 ch (counts as dc (*UK tr*)), skip next st, 3 dc (*UK 3 tr*) in ch sp, *skip next 2 sts, 3 dc (*UK 3 tr*) in ch sp, rep from * across, dc (*UK tr*) in top of 2-ch. Turn.

Row 3: 2 ch (counts as hdc (*UK htr*)), skip next st, [sc (*UK dc*), 2 ch, sc (*UK dc*)] into next st, *skip 2 sts, [sc (*UK dc*), 2 ch, sc (*UK dc*)] in next st, rep from * until 2 sts rem, skip next st, hdc (*UK htr*) in top of 3-ch. Turn.

Rep Rows 2 and 3 until desired height.

Fasten off and sew in ends.

Little Fans

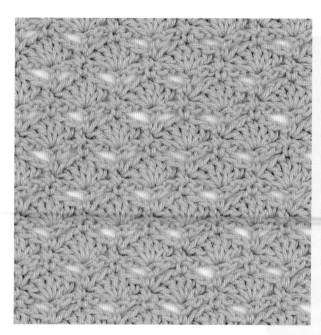

Skill level
Beginner

Multiples
6 + 2

Stitches used
ch, sc (*UK dc*), dc (*UK tr*),
ShSt – see 'Special stitch' below

Special stitch
ShSt = Shell Stitch: work 5 dc (*UK 5 tr*)
in indicated stitch

Colour
Blush Pink

INSTRUCTIONS

Row 1: sc (*UK dc*) in second ch from hook (skipped ch does not count as st), *skip 2 ch, ShSt in next ch, skip 2 ch, sc (*UK dc*) in next ch, rep from * across. Turn.

Row 2: 5 ch (counts as dc (*UK tr*) and 2-ch), *sc (*UK dc*) in middle dc (*UK tr*) of next ShSt, 2 ch, dc (*UK tr*) in next sc (*UK dc*), 2 ch, rep from * across, omitting last 2 ch on final rep. Turn.

Row 3: 3 ch (counts as a dc (*UK tr*)), 2 dc (*UK 2 tr*) in same st as 3-ch, skip ch sp, sc (*UK dc*) in next st, *skip ch sp, ShSt in next dc (*UK tr*), skip ch sp, sc (*UK dc*) in next st, rep from * across to last ch sp, 3 dc (*UK tr*) in third ch of 5-ch. Turn.

Row 4: 3 ch (counts as sc (*UK dc*) and 2-ch), *skip 2 sts, dc (*UK tr*) in next sc (*UK dc*), 2 ch, skip 2 sts, sc (*UK dc*) in centre dc (*UK tr*) of ShSt, 2 ch, rep from * across, working last sc (*UK dc*) in top of 3-ch and omitting last 2 ch. Turn.

Row 5: 1 ch (does not count as st), sc (*UK dc*) in first st, *skip ch sp, ShSt in next dc (*UK tr*), skip ch sp, sc (*UK dc*) in next st, rep from * across, working last sc (*UK dc*) in last ch. Turn.

Rep Rows 2–5 until desired height.

Fasten off and sew in ends.

Herringbone Double Crochet

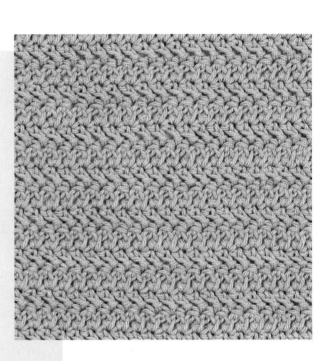

Skill level
Beginner

Multiples
1 + 1

Stitches used
ch, HBdc (*UK HBtr*) – see 'Special stitch' below

Special stitch
**HBdc (*UK HBtr*) = Herringbone Double Crochet
(*UK Herringbone Treble Crochet*):** yo, insert hook
into st, yo, pull through st and first loop on hook, yo,
pull through first loop, yo, pull through rem 2 loops
on the hook

Colour
Stormy Grey

INSTRUCTIONS

Row 1: HBdc (*UK HBtr*) in fourth ch from hook (skipped 3-ch
counts as st), HBdc (*UK HBtr*) in each ch across. Turn.

Row 2: 3 ch (counts as st here and throughout), HBdc (*UK HBtr*)
in each st across. Turn.

Rep Row 2 until desired height.

Fasten off and sew in ends.

Block

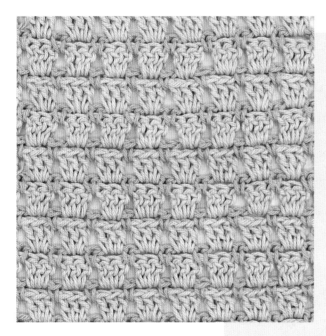

Skill level
Beginner

Multiples
3 + 2

Stitches used
ch, dc (*UK tr*), sc (*UK dc*)
Ssc (*UK Sdc*) – see 'Special stitch' below

Special stitch
Ssc (*UK Sdc*) = Standing Single Crochet (*UK Standing Double Crochet*): with slip knot on the hook, insert hook into stitch, yo, pull up a loop (2 loops on hook), yo, pull through rem 2 loops on the hook

Pattern note
Standing stitches, such as SSc (*UK Sdc*), create neater colour changes than the usual method of starting with a slip stitch and chain stitch.

Colours
Vanilla Cream (A), Pistachio Green (B)

INSTRUCTIONS

Row 1: with yarn A dc (*UK tr*) in fifth ch from hook (skipped 4-ch counts as st), dc (*UK tr*) in each ch across. Do not turn your work.

Pull up the working loop, remove your hook and add a stitch marker to the loop so you don't lose it.

Row 2: join in yarn B with a Ssc (*UK Sdc*) in sp between turning ch and dc (*UK tr*) from previous row, *2 ch, skip 3 sts, sc (*UK dc*) in next sp between dc (*UK tr*), rep from * across, working last st into last sp before final st. Fasten off yarn B. Turn.

Row 3: remove stitch marker from loop of yarn A and insert hook, 3 ch (counts as dc (*UK tr*)), *3 dc (*UK tr*) in next ch sp, rep from * across, dc (*UK tr*) in top of turning ch from two rows below. Do not turn your work.

Pull up the working loop, remove your hook and add a stitch marker as previously.

Rep Rows 2 and 3 until desired height.

Fasten off and sew in ends.

Brick

Skill level
Beginner

Multiples
4 + 2

Stitches used
ch, sc (*UK dc*), SSp – see 'Special stitch' below

Special stitch
SSp = Stretched Spike Stitch: sc (*UK dc*) into st
three rows below

Colours
Stormy Grey (A), Sea Foam (B)

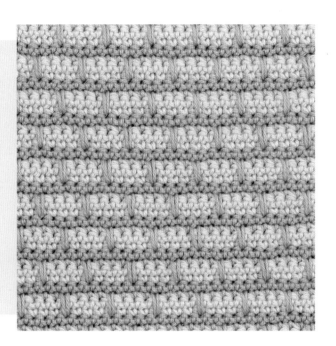

INSTRUCTIONS

Row 1: with yarn A, sc (*UK dc*) in second ch from hook
(skipped ch does not count as st), sc (*UK dc*) in each
ch across. Turn.

Row 2: 1 ch (does not count as st here or throughout),
sc (*UK dc*) in each st across, changing to yarn B in last
yo of last st. Turn.

Rows 3 and 4: 1 ch, sc (*UK dc*) in each st across,
changing to yarn A in last yo of last st of Row 4. Turn.

Row 5: 1 ch, sc (*UK dc*) in first 2 sts, *SSp in next st,
sc (*UK dc*) in next 3 sts, rep from * until 3 sts rem,
SSp, sc (*UK dc*) in last 2 sts. Turn.

Rows 6–8: rep Rows 2–4.

Row 9: 1 ch, *SSp in next st, sc (*UK dc*) in next 3 sts,
rep from * until 1 st rem, SSp in last st. Turn.

Rep Rows 2–9 until desired height.

Fasten off and sew in ends.

Leaping Stripes

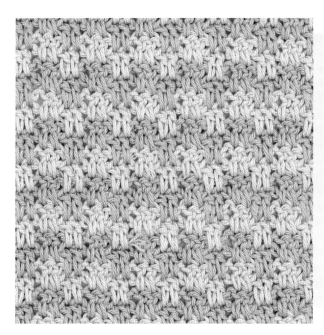

Skill level
Beginner

Multiples
4 + 2

Stitches used
ch, dc (*UK tr*), sc (*UK dc*)

Colours
Vanilla Cream (A), Pistachio Green (B)

INSTRUCTIONS

Row 1: with yarn A dc (*UK tr*) in fourth ch from hook (skipped 3-ch counts as a dc (*UK tr*)), dc (*UK tr*) in next ch, *2 ch, skip 2 ch, dc (*UK tr*) in next 2 ch, rep from * until 1 ch rem, work dc (*UK tr*) in last ch. Turn.

Row 2: 1 ch (does not count as st here or throughout), sc (*UK dc*) in first st, 2 ch, skip next 2 dc (*UK 2 tr*), *working over ch sp from Row 1, dc (*UK tr*) in next skipped 2-ch from foundation ch, 2 ch, skip next 2 dc (*UK 2 tr*), rep from * across, sc (*UK dc*) in top of 3-ch changing to yarn B in last yo of last st. Turn.

Row 3: 1 ch, sc (*UK dc*) in first st, working over ch sp from previous row dc (*UK tr*) in top of next 2 dc (*UK 2 tr*) from two rows below, *2 ch, skip 2 sts from previous row, dc (*UK tr*) in top of next 2 dc (*UK 2 tr*) from two rows below, rep from * until 1 st rem, sc (*UK dc*) in last st. Turn.

Row 4: 1 ch, sc (*UK dc*) in first st, 2 ch, skip 2 dc (*UK 2 tr*) from previous row, *working over ch sp from previous row dc (*UK tr*) in next 2 dc (*UK 2 tr*) from two rows below, 2 ch, skip 2 dc (*UK 2 tr*) from previous row, rep from * until 1 st rem, sc (*UK dc*) in last st, changing to yarn A in last yo of last st. Turn.

Rep Rows 3 and 4, alternating colours every two rows, until desired height.

Fasten off and sew in ends.

Eyelet

Skill level
Beginner

Multiples
4 + 2

Stitches used
ch, sc (*UK dc*)

Colour
Sea Foam

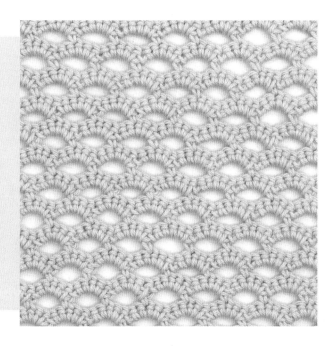

INSTRUCTIONS

Row 1: sc (*UK dc*) in second ch from hook (skipped ch does not count as st), *3 ch, skip 3 chs, sc (*UK dc*) in next ch, rep from * across. Turn.

Row 2: 1 ch (does not count as st here and throughout), skip sc (*UK dc*), 5 sc (*UK 5 dc*) in ch sp, *skip sc (*UK dc*), 5 sc (*UK 5 dc*) in ch sp, rep from * to last ch sp, 4 sc (*UK 4 dc*) in ch sp, sc (*UK dc*) in last st. Turn.

Row 3: 3 ch (counts as sc (*UK dc*) and 2 ch), skip st at base of 3-ch and next st, sc (*UK dc*) in next st, *3 ch, skip next 4 sts, sc (*UK dc*) in next st, rep from * until 2 sts rem, 2 ch, skip 1 st, sc (*UK dc*) in last st. Turn.

Row 4: 1 ch, 3 sc (*UK 3 dc*) in ch sp, *skip next st, 5 sc (*UK 5 dc*) in ch sp, rep from * to beginning 3-ch sp, skip last sc (*UK dc*), 2 sc (*UK 2 dc*) in 3-ch sp, sc (*UK dc*) in third ch of beginning 3-ch. Turn.

Row 5: 1 ch, sc (*UK dc*) in first st, *3 ch, skip 4 sts, sc (*UK dc*) in next st, rep from * across. Turn.

Rep Rows 2–5 until desired height.

Fasten off and sew in ends.

Rolling Waves

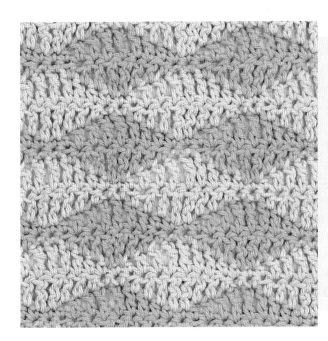

Skill level
Beginner

Multiples
10 + 3

Stitches used
ch, sc (*UK dc*), dc (*UK tr*), hdc (*UK htr*), tr (*UK dtr*)

Colours
Vanilla Cream (A), Blush Pink (B)

INSTRUCTIONS

Row 1: with yarn A sc (*UK dc*) in second ch from hook (skipped ch does not count as st), *sc (*UK dc*) in next ch, hdc (*UK htr*) in next ch, dc (*UK tr*) in next 2 ch, tr (*UK dtr*) in next 2 ch, dc (*UK tr*) in next 2 ch, hdc (*UK htr*) in next ch, sc (*UK dc*) in next ch, rep from * until 1 ch rem, sc (*UK dc*) in last ch, changing to yarn B in last yo of last st. Turn.

Row 2: 4 ch (counts as a dc (*UK tr*) here and throughout), *tr (*UK dtr*) in next st, dc (*UK tr*) in next 2 sts, hdc (*UK htr*) in next st, sc (*UK dc*) in next 2 sts, hdc (*UK htr*) in next st, dc (*UK tr*) in next 2 sts, tr (*UK dtr*) in next st, rep from * until 1 st rem, tr (*UK dtr*) in last st. Turn.

Row 3: rep Row 2, changing to yarn A in last yo of last st. Turn.

Row 4: 1 ch (does not count as a st here and throughout), sc (*UK dc*) in first st, *sc (*UK dc*) in next st, hdc (*UK htr*) in next st, dc (*UK tr*) in next 2 sts, tr (*UK dtr*) in next 2 sts, dc (*UK tr*) in next 2 sts, hdc (*UK htr*) in next st, sc (*UK dc*) in next st, rep from * until 1 st rem, sc (*UK dc*) in last st. Turn.

Row 5: rep Row 4, changing to yarn B in last yo of last st. Turn.

Rep Rows 2–5 until desired height.

Fasten off and sew in ends.

Bead

Skill level
Intermediate

Multiples
2 + 1

Stitches used
ch, sc (*UK dc*), dc (*UK tr*),
bst – see 'Special stitch' below

Special stitch
bst = Bead Stitch: [yo, insert the hook behind
the previous dc (*UK tr*) from front to back, yo and
pull through a loop] three times around the same
dc (*UK tr*) (7 loops on hook), yo and pull through
6 loops, yo and pull through rem loops on the hook

Pattern note
When working your bead stitch, do not pull the
yarn too tight as this can make the stitch difficult
to complete.

Colour
Sea Foam

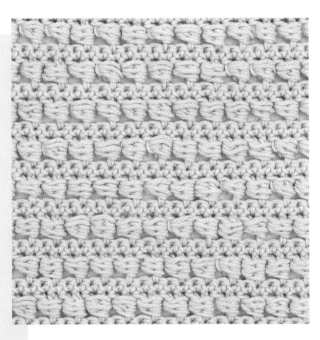

INSTRUCTIONS

Row 1: sc (*UK dc*) in second ch from the hook
(skipped ch does not count as st), sc (*UK dc*) in each
ch across. Turn.

Row 2: 3 ch (counts as dc (*UK tr*)), *dc (*UK tr*) in
next st, bst around post of dc (*UK tr*) just made,
skip sc (*UK dc*), rep from * across until 1 st rem,
dc (*UK tr*) in last stitch. Turn.

Row 3: 1 ch (does not count as st), sc (*UK dc*) in each
dc (*UK tr*) and bst across. Turn.

Rep Rows 2 and 3 until desired height, ending with
a Row 3.

Fasten off and sew in ends.

Blocked Bead

INSTRUCTIONS

Row 1: sc (*UK dc*) in third ch from hook (skipped 2-ch counts as esc (*UK edc*)), sc (*UK dc*) in next ch, esc (*UK edc*) in next ch, *sc (*UK dc*) in next 2 ch, esc (*UK edc*) in next ch, rep from * across. Turn.

Row 2: 2 ch (counts as an esc (*UK edc*) here and throughout), *dc (*UK tr*) in next st, Abs around post of dc (*UK tr*) just made, skip next sc (*UK dc*), esc (*UK edc*) in next st, rep from * across working last esc (*UK edc*) in top of 2-ch. Turn.

Row 3: 2 ch, *sc (*UK dc*) into top of Abs, sc (*UK dc*) in next st, esc (*UK edc*) in next st, rep from * across, working last esc (*UK edc*) in top of 2-ch. Turn.

Rep Rows 2 and 3 until desired height.

Fasten off and sew in ends.

Skill level
Intermediate

Multiples
3 + 2

Stitches used
ch, sc (*UK dc*), esc (*UK edc*) – see 'Special stitches' below, dc (*UK tr*), Abs – see 'Special stitches' below

Special stitches
esc (*UK edc*) = Extended Single Crochet (*UK Extended Double Crochet*): insert hook into st or sp, yo, pull up a loop, yo, pull through 1 loop only, yo, pull through both loops on hook

Abs = Alternative Bead Stitch (Abs): [yo, insert the hook behind the previous dc (*UK tr*) from front to back, yo and pull through a loop] three times around the same dc (*UK tr*) (7 loops on hook), yo and pull through rem 7 loops on the hook

Pattern note
When working your bead stitch, do not pull the yarn too tight as this can make the stitch difficult to complete.

Colour
Blush Pink

Arcade

Skill level
Intermediate

Multiples
6 + 2

Stitches used
ch, sc (*UK dc*), dc (*UK tr*)

Colour
Pistachio Green

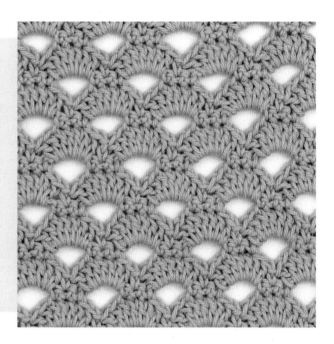

INSTRUCTIONS

Row 1: sc (*UK dc*) in second ch from hook (skipped ch does not count as st), sc (*UK dc*) in next st, 3 ch, skip 3 sts, *3 sc (*UK 3 dc*), 3 ch, skip 3 ch, rep from * until 2 ch rem, sc (*UK dc*) in next 2 ch. Turn.

Row 2: 1 ch (does not count as st here and throughout), skip 2 sts, 7 dc (*UK 7 tr*) in ch sp, *skip next st, sc (*UK dc*) in next st, skip next st, 7 dc (*UK 7 tr*) in ch sp, rep from * until 2 sts rem, skip next st, sc (*UK dc*) in last st. Turn.

Row 3: 4 ch (counts as ch sp), skip 3 sts, sc (*UK dc*) in next 3 sts (this will be the middle 3 sts of prev 7-dc (*UK 7-tr*) 'fan'), *3 ch, skip 5 sts, sc (*UK dc*) in next 3 sts, rep from * until 2 sts rem, 1 ch, skip next st, dc (*UK tr*) in last st (1 ch and dc (*UK tr*) count as ch sp). Turn.

Row 4: 3 ch (counts as dc (*UK tr*)), work 3 dc (*UK 3 tr*) in next ch sp, skip next st, sc (*UK dc*) in next st, skip next st, *7 dc (*UK 7 tr*) in ch sp, skip next st, sc (*UK dc*) in next st, skip next st, rep from * to last ch sp, 4 dc (*UK 4 tr*) in last ch sp. Turn.

Row 5: 1 ch, sc (*UK dc*) in next 2 sts, 3 ch, skip 5 sts, *sc (*UK dc*) in next 3 sts, 3 ch, skip 5 sts, rep from * until 2 sts rem, sc (*UK dc*) in next st, sc (*UK dc*) in top of 3-ch. Turn.

Rep Rows 2–5 until desired height.

Fasten off and sew in ends.

Cluster

Skill level
Intermediate

Multiples
2 + 2

Stitches used
ch, sc (*UK dc*), CS – see 'Special stitches' below, dc (*UK tr*)

Special stitch
CS = Cluster Stitch: [yo, insert hook, yo and pull up a loop, yo and pull through 2 loops on the hook] three times, yo and pull through rem 4 loops on the hook

Colour
Blush Pink

INSTRUCTIONS

Row 1: sc (*UK dc*) in second ch from hook (skipped ch does not count as st), sc (*UK dc*) in next ch, *1 ch, skip 1 ch, sc (*UK dc*) in next ch, rep from * until 3 ch remaining, 1 ch, skip 1 ch, sc (*UK dc*) in last 2 ch. Turn.

Row 2: 4 ch (counts as dc (*UK tr*) and 1 ch), skip st at base of 4-ch and next st, CS in ch sp, *1 ch, skip sc (*UK dc*), CS in ch sp, rep from * until 2 sts rem, 1 ch, skip sc (*UK dc*), dc (*UK tr*) in last st. Turn.

Row 3: 1 ch (does not count as st), sc (*UK dc*) in first st, sc (*UK dc*) in ch sp before first cluster, *1 ch, sc (*UK dc*) in next ch sp between clusters, rep from * across working final sc (*UK dc*) in fourth ch of initial 4-ch, sc (*UK dc*) in third ch of 4-ch. Turn.

Rep Rows 2 and 3 until desired height.

Fasten off and sew in ends.

Crossed Treble

Skill level
Intermediate

Multiples
2 + 2

Stitches used
ch, CDC (*UK CTR*) – see 'Special stitch' below,
dc (*UK tr*), sc (*UK dc*)

Special stitch
**CDC (UK CTR) = Crossed Double Crochet
(*UK Crossed Treble Crochet*):** skip next st, dc (*UK tr*)
into next st, dc (*UK tr*) into skipped st working over
the previous dc (*UK tr*)

Colour
Vanilla Cream

INSTRUCTIONS

Row 1: skip 3 ch (skipped 3-ch counts as dc (*UK tr*)),
[CDC (*UK CTR*) over next 2 ch] until 1 ch rem,
dc (*UK tr*) in last ch. Turn.

Row 2: 1 ch (does not count as st here or
throughout), sc (*UK dc*) in each st across. Turn.

Row 3: 3 ch (counts as dc (*UK tr*)), CDC (*UK CTR*)
across until 1 st rem, dc (*UK tr*) in last st. Turn.

Row 4: 1 ch, sc (*UK dc*) in each st across. Turn.

Rep Rows 3 and 4 until desired height.

Fasten off and sew in ends.

Thermal

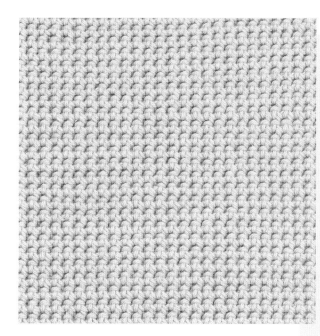

INSTRUCTIONS

Row 1: sc (*UK dc*) in BLO of second ch from hook (skipped ch does not count as st), sc (*UK dc*) in BLO of each ch across. Turn.

Row 2: 1 ch (does not count as st here or throughout), SThs in each st across. Turn.

Row 3: 1 ch, Ths in each st across. Turn.
Rep Row 3 until desired height.

Final Row: 1 ch, CThs in each st across.
Fasten off and sew in ends.

Skill level
Intermediate

Multiples
1 + 2

Stitches used
ch, sc (*UK dc*), SThs – see 'Special stitches' below, Ths – see 'Special stitches' below, CThs – see 'Special stitches' below

Special stitches
SThs = Starting Thermal Stitch: insert hook into BLO of next st PLUS the unworked loop on foundation ch, yo and pull up a loop, yo, pull through rem loops on the hook

Ths = Thermal Stitch: insert hook into BLO of next st PLUS the unworked loop on the row below, yo and pull up a loop, yo, pull through rem loops on the hook

CThs = Closing Thermal Stitch: insert hook into both loops of next st PLUS the unworked loop on the row below, yo and pull up a loop, yo, pull through rem loops on the hook

Pattern note
Refer to page 172 for more information on BLO.

Colour
Sea Foam

Spike

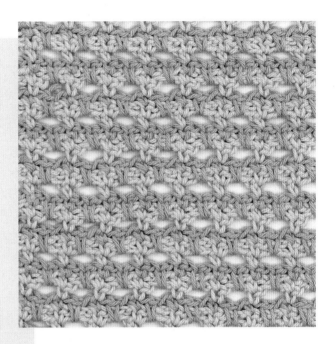

Skill level
Intermediate

Multiples
4 + 4

Stitches used
ch, sc (*UK dc*), SpSt – see 'Special stitch' below

Special stitch
SpSt = Spike Stitch: sc (*UK dc*) into st or ch sp two rows below

Colours
Vanilla Cream (A), Pistachio Green (B)

INSTRUCTIONS

Row 1: sc (*UK dc*) in second ch from hook (skipped ch does not count as st), *sc (*UK dc*) in next st, 3 ch, skip 3 ch, rep from * until 2 ch rem, sc (*UK dc*) in last 2 ch. Turn.

Row 2: 1 ch (does not count as st here or throughout), sc (*UK dc*) in first 2 sts, *3 ch, skip ch sp, sc (*UK dc*) in next sc (*UK dc*), rep from * until 1 st rem, sc (*UK dc*) in last st changing to yarn B in last yo. Turn.

Row 3: 1 ch, sc (*UK dc*) in first 2 sts, *1 ch, SpSt, 1 ch, sc (*UK dc*) in next st, rep from * until 1 st rem, sc (*UK dc*) in last st, changing to yarn A in last yo. Turn.

Row 4: 1 ch, sc (*UK dc*) in first 2 sts, *3 ch, skip SpSt, sc (*UK dc*) in next sc (*UK dc*), rep from * until 1 st rem, sc (*UK dc*) in last st. Turn.

Row 5: rep Row 2.

Rep Rows 3–5 until desired height.

Fasten off and sew in ends.

Alternating Spike

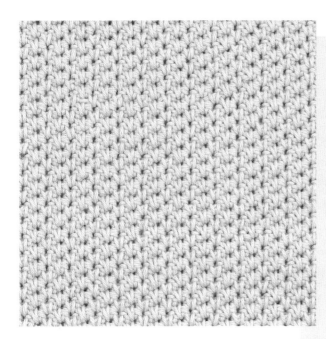

Skill level
Intermediate

Multiples
2 + 1

Stitches used
ch, sc (*UK dc*), SpSt – see 'Special stitch' below

Special stitch
SpSt = Spike Stitch: sc (*UK dc*) into st or ch sp two rows below

Colour
Sea Foam

INSTRUCTIONS

Row 1: sc (*UK dc*) in second ch from hook (skipped ch does not count as st), sc (*UK dc*) in each ch across. Turn.

Row 2: 1 ch (does not count as st here or throughout), *sc (*UK dc*) in next st, SpSt (working into foundation ch), rep from * until 2 sts rem, sc (*UK dc*) in last 2 sts. Turn.

Row 3: 1 ch, *sc (*UK dc*) in next st, SpSt, rep from * until 2 sts rem, sc (*UK dc*) in last 2 sts. Turn.

Rep Row 3 until desired height.

Fasten off and sew in ends.

Triangle

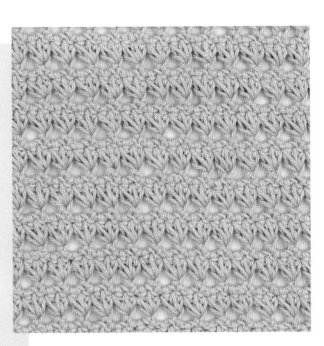

Skill level
Intermediate

Multiples
2 + 1

Stitches used
ch, sc (*UK dc*), TS – see 'Special stitch' below, hdc (*UK htr*)

Special stitch
TS = Triangle Stitch: yo, insert hook into first st as directed, yo and pull through a loop (3 loops on hook), yo, insert hook into next st, yo and pull through a loop (5 loops on hook), yo, insert hook into next st, yo and pull through a loop (7 loops on hook), yo and pull through rem loops on the hook

Colour
Vanilla Cream

INSTRUCTIONS

Row 1: sc (*UK dc*) in second ch and each ch across. Turn.

Row 2: 3 ch (counts as hdc (*UK htr*) and 1 ch), starting in first sc (*UK dc*) at base of 3-ch, *TS, 2 ch, beginning in last worked st of previous TS st, rep from * until 1 st rem, hdc (*UK htr*) in last st. Turn.

Row 3: 1 ch (does not count as st), sc (*UK dc*) in first st and ch sp, *skip TS, work 2 sc (*UK 2 dc*) in ch sp, rep from * until 1 ch sp rem, sc (*UK dc*) in ch sp, sc (*UK dc*) in second ch of 3-ch. Turn.

Rep Rows 2 and 3 until desired height.

Fasten off and sew in ends.

Double Linen/Moss

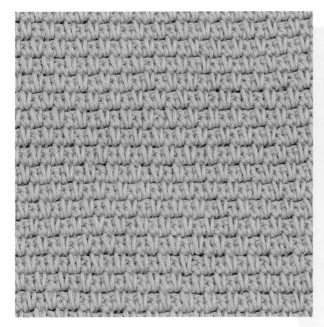

Skill level
Intermediate

Multiples
2 + 2

Stitches used
ch, sc (*UK dc*), SpSt – see 'Special stitch' below

Special stitch
SpSt = Spike Stitch: sc (*UK dc*) into st or ch sp two rows below

Colours
Blush Pink

INSTRUCTIONS

Row 1: sc (*UK dc*) in second ch from hook (skipped ch does not count as st), sc (*UK dc*) in each ch across. Turn.

Row 2: 1 ch (does not count as st here or throughout), sc (*UK dc*) in first st, *1 ch, skip next st, sc (*UK dc*) in next st, rep from * across. Turn.

Row 3: 1 ch, sc (*UK dc*) in first st, *1 ch, skip next ch sp, sc (*UK dc*) in next st, rep from * across. Turn.

Row 4: 1 ch, sc (*UK dc*) in first st, SpSt, *1 ch, skip next st, SpSt, rep from * until 1 st rem, sc (*UK dc*) in last st. Turn.

Row 5: 1 ch, sc (*UK dc*) in next 2 sts, *1 ch, skip next ch sp, sc (*UK dc*) in next st, rep from * to last st, sc (*UK dc*) in last st. Turn.

Row 6: 1 ch, sc (*UK dc*) in first st, *1 ch, skip next st, SpSt, rep from * until 2 sts rem, 1 ch, skip next st, sc (*UK dc*) in last st. Turn.

Rep Rows 3–6 until desired height.

Fasten off and sew in ends.

Twin Cluster

Skill level
Intermediate

Multiples
3 + 3

Stitches used
ch, sc (*UK dc*), dc (*UK tr*),
TC – see 'Special stitch' below

Special stitch
TC = Twin Cluster Stitch: [yo, insert hook into next st,
yo and pull through, yo and pull through 2 loops on
the hook] three times into the SAME sc (*UK dc*), skip
the next sc (*UK dc*), [yo, insert hook into next st, yo
and pull through, yo and pull through 2 loops on the
hook] three times into the SAME sc (*UK dc*), yo and
pull through rem 7 loops on the hook

Colour
Stormy Grey

INSTRUCTIONS

Row 1: sc (*UK dc*) in second ch from hook (skipped ch
does not count as st), sc (*UK dc*) in each ch across. Turn.
Row 2: 4 ch (counts as a dc (*UK tr*) and 1 ch), *TC over next
3 sts, 2 ch, rep from * until 1 st rem, dc (*UK tr*) in last st.
Turn.
Row 3: 1 ch (does not count as st), sc (*UK dc*) in first st,
sc (*UK dc*) in ch sp, *sc (*UK dc*) in top of TC, 2 sc (*UK 2 dc*)
in ch sp, rep from * until 1 TC remaining, sc (*UK dc*) in
top of TC, sc (*UK dc*) in ch sp, sc (*UK dc*) in third ch of
4-ch. Turn.
Rep Rows 2 and 3 until desired height.
Fasten off and sew in ends.

Forked Cluster

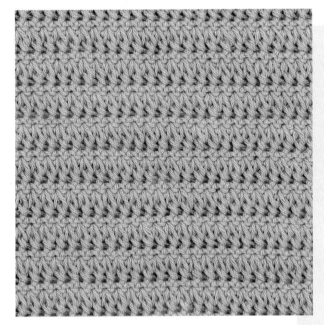

Skill level
Intermediate

Multiples
1 + 4

Stitches used
ch, Ffc – see 'Special stitches' below, fc – see 'Special stitches' below, dc (*UK tr*), sc (*UK dc*)

Special stitches
Ffc = First Forked Cluster Stitch: yo, insert hook into indicated st, pull up a loop (3 loops on hook), yo, insert hook into the next st, pull up a loop (5 loops on hook), yo, pull through 3 loops (3 loops on hook), yo, pull through rem 3 loops on the hook

fc = Forked Cluster Stitch: yo, insert hook into the same st as last st made, pull up a loop (3 loops on hook), yo, insert hook into the next st, pull up a loop (5 loops on hook), yo, pull through 3 loops (3 loops on hook), yo, pull through rem 3 loops on the hook

Colour
Pistachio Green

INSTRUCTIONS

Row 1: Ffc in fourth ch from hook (skipped 3-ch does not count as st), fc across, dc (*UK tr*) in same st as last st made. Turn.

Row 2: 1 ch (does not count as st), sc (*UK dc*) in each st across. Turn.

Row 3: 3 ch (does not count as st), starting in first st, Ffc, fc across, dc (*UK tr*) in same st as last st made. Turn.

Rep Rows 2 and 3 until desired height.

Fasten off and sew in ends.

Little Arches

Skill level
Intermediate

Multiples
4 + 4

Stitches used
ch, sc (*UK dc*)

Colour
Stormy Grey

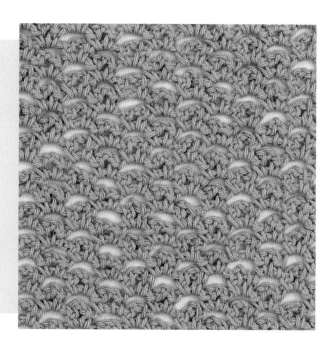

INSTRUCTIONS

Row 1: sc (*UK dc*) in fourth ch from hook (skipped 3-ch counts as 3-ch sp), *3 ch, sc (*UK dc*) in next ch, 3 ch, skip 2 ch, sc (*UK dc*) in next ch, rep from * across. Turn.

Row 2: 3 ch, skip first sc (*UK dc*), *[sc (*UK dc*), 3 ch, sc (*UK dc*)] in 3-ch sp, 3 ch, skip [sc (*UK dc*), 3-ch sp, sc (*UK dc*)], rep from * across, sc (*UK dc*) in beginning 3-ch sp. Turn.

Rep Row 2 until desired height.

Final row: 1 ch, sc (*UK dc*) in first st, *1 ch, sc (*UK dc*) in next 3-ch sp, rep from * across until one 3-ch sp rem, 1 ch, sc (*UK dc*) in 3-ch sp.

Fasten off and sew in ends.

Filet

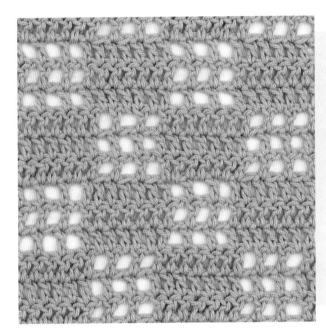

Skill level
Intermediate

Multiples
12 + 3

Stitches used
ch, dc (*UK tr*)

Colour
Pistachio Green

INSTRUCTIONS

Row 1: dc (*UK tr*) in fourth ch from hook (skipped 3-ch counts as dc (*UK tr*)), dc (*UK tr*) in next 5 ch, *[1 ch, skip next ch, dc (*UK tr*) in next ch] three times**, dc (*UK tr*) in next 6 ch, rep from * across, ending last rep at **. Turn.

Row 2: 4 ch (counts as dc (*UK tr*) and 1 ch), [skip ch sp, dc (*UK tr*) in next st, 1 ch] twice, skip ch sp, *dc (*UK tr*) in next 6 sts**, [dc (*UK tr*) in next st, 1 ch, skip ch sp] three times, rep from *, ending last rep at ** with 1 st rem, dc (*UK tr*) in top of 3-ch. Turn.

Row 3: 3 ch (counts as dc (*UK tr*) here and throughout), *dc (*UK tr*) in next 6 sts, [1 ch, skip ch sp, dc (*UK tr*) in next st] three times, rep from * across, ending with final dc (*UK tr*) in third ch of 4-ch. Turn.

Row 4: 3 ch, *[dc (*UK tr*) in ch sp, dc (*UK tr*) in next st] three times, [1 ch, skip next st, dc (*UK tr*) in next st] three times, rep from * across, ending with final dc (*UK tr*) in top of 3-ch. Turn.

Row 5: 3 ch, *[1 ch, skip ch sp, dc (*UK tr*) in next st] three times, dc (*UK tr*) in next 6 sts, rep from * across, ending with final dc (*UK tr*) in top of 3-ch. Turn.

Row 6: rep Row 3.

Row 7: rep Row 4.

Rep Rows 2–7 until desired height.

Fasten off and sew in ends.

Sturdy Mesh

Skill level
Intermediate

Multiples
4 + 3

Stitches used
ch, sc (*UK dc*), dc (*UK tr*)

Colour
Blush Pink

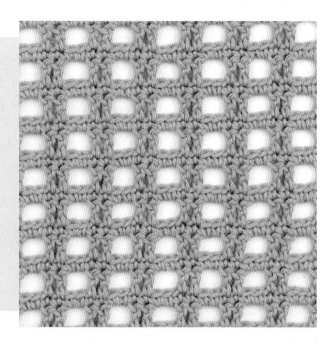

INSTRUCTIONS

Row 1: sc (*UK dc*) in second ch from hook (skipped ch does not count as st), sc (*UK dc*) in each ch across. Turn.

Row 2: 3 ch (counts as dc (*UK tr*) here and throughout), dc (*UK tr*) in next st, *2 ch, skip 2 sts, dc (*UK tr*) in next 2 sts, rep from * across. Turn.

Row 3: 1 ch (does not count as st here or throughout), sc (*UK dc*) in first 2 sts, *2 sc (*UK 2 dc*) in ch sp, sc (*UK dc*) in next 2 sts, rep from * to end. Turn.

Rep Rows 2 and 3 until desired height.

Fasten off and sew in ends.

Colander

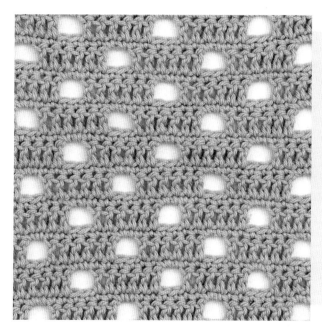

Skill level
Intermediate

Multiples
8 + 1

Stitches used
ch, sc (*UK dc*), dc (*UK tr*)

Colour
Stormy Grey

INSTRUCTIONS

Row 1: sc (*UK dc*) in second ch from hook (skipped ch does not count as st), sc (*UK dc*) in each ch across. Turn.

Row 2: 3 ch (counts as dc (*UK tr*) here and throughout), *dc (*UK tr*) in next 6 sts, 2 ch, skip 2 sts, rep from * until 7 sts rem, dc (*UK tr*) in last 7 sts. Turn.

Row 3: 1 ch (does not count as st here or throughout), sc (*UK dc*) in next 7 sts, *2 sc (*UK 2 dc*) in ch sp, sc (*UK dc*) in next 6 sts, rep from * until 1 st rem, sc (*UK dc*) in top of 3-ch. Turn.

Row 4: 3 ch, dc (*UK tr*) in next 2 sts, 2 ch, skip 2 sts, *dc (*UK tr*) in next 6 sts, 2 ch, skip 2 sts, rep from * until 3 sts rem, dc (*UK tr*) in last 3 sts. Turn.

Row 5: 1 ch, sc (*UK dc*) in next 3 sts, 2 sc (*UK 2 dc*) in ch sp, *sc (*UK dc*) in next 6 sts, 2 sc (*UK 2 dc*) in ch sp, rep from * until 3 sts rem, sc (*UK dc*) in each of the last 3 sts. Turn.

Rep Rows 2–5 until desired height.

Fasten off and sew in ends.

Chevron

Skill level
Intermediate

Multiples
25 + 5

Stitches used
ch, sc (*UK dc*)

Pattern note
This sample is made with three colours changing every two rows; however, it can be made in any number of colours, which can change in any number of rows.

Colours
Vanilla Cream (A), Sea Foam (B), Blush Pink (C)

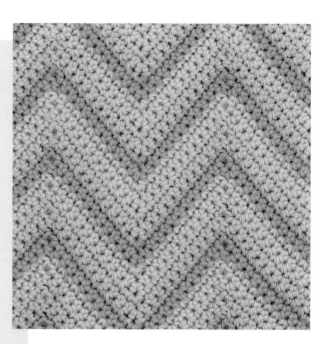

INSTRUCTIONS

Row 1: with yarn A sc (*UK dc*) in second ch from hook (skipped ch does not count as st), sc (*UK dc*) in next ch, *skip 1 ch, sc (*UK dc*) in next 11 ch, 3 sc (*UK 3 dc*) in next ch, sc (*UK dc*) in next 11 ch, skip 1 ch, rep from * across until 2 ch rem, sc (*UK dc*) in last 2 ch. Turn.

Row 2: 1 ch (does not count as st), sc (*UK dc*) in first 2 sts, *skip 1 st, sc (*UK dc*) in next 11 sts, 3 sc (*UK 3 dc*) in next st, sc (*UK dc*) in next 11 sts, skip 1 st, rep from * across until 2 sts rem, sc (*UK dc*) in last 2 sts, changing to yarn B in last yo of last st. Turn.

Rep Row 2 until desired height, changing to the next colour every two rows.

Fasten off and sew in ends.

Side Saddle

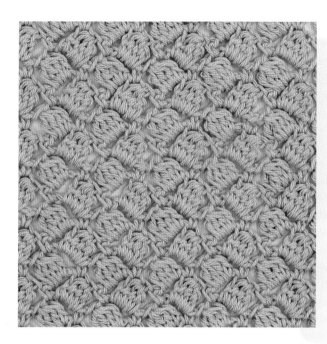

Skill level
Intermediate

Multiples
5 + 2

Stitches used
ch, sc (*UK dc*), dc (*UK tr*)

Pattern note
After Row 2, dc4tog (*UK tr4tog*) will be referred to as 'cluster.'

Colour
Stormy Grey

INSTRUCTIONS

Row 1: sc (*UK dc*) in second ch from hook (skipped ch does not count as st), *3 ch, dc4tog (*UK tr4tog*) over next 4 ch, 1 ch (this secures the cluster), sc (*UK dc*) into next ch, rep from * across. Turn.

Row 2: 5 ch (counts as ch sp), *sc (*UK dc*) in top of dc4tog (*UK tr4tog*) cluster from previous row, 3 ch, dc4tog (*UK tr4tog*) into 3-ch sp from previous row, 1 ch, rep from * across until 1 st rem, dc (*UK tr*) in last st. Turn.

Row 3: 1 ch (does not count as st), skip first st, sc (*UK dc*) into top of first cluster, *3 ch, dc4tog (*UK tr4tog*) into ch sp from previous row, 1 ch, sc (*UK dc*) into top of next cluster, rep from * working final sc (*UK dc*) in ch sp. Turn.

Rep Rows 2 and 3 until desired height.

Fasten off and sew in ends.

Granny Spike

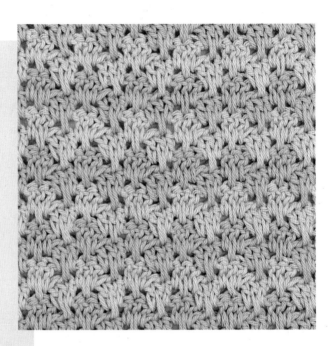

Skill level
Intermediate

Multiples
4 + 1

Stitches used
ch, dc (*UK tr*), SpDc (*UK SpTr*) –
see 'Special stitch' below

Special stitch
**SpDc (*UK SpTr*) = Spike Double Crochet
(*UK Spike Treble Crochet*):** dc (*UK tr*) into
indicated st two rows below

Colours
Pistachio Green (A), Vanilla Cream (B)

INSTRUCTIONS

Row 1: with yarn A work 3 dc (*UK 3 tr*) in fifth ch from
hook (skipped 4-ch counts as a st), *1 ch, skip 3 ch,
3 dc (*UK 3 tr*) in next ch, rep from * until 4 ch rem, 1 ch,
skip 3 ch, dc (*UK tr*) in last ch. Turn.

Row 2: 2 ch (counts as st here and throughout),
*[dc (*UK tr*), SpDc (*UK SpTr*) in middle ch of skipped
chs from two rows below, dc (*UK tr*)] in 1-ch sp, 1 ch,
skip 3 sts, rep from * until 1 st rem, dc (*UK tr*) in top of
4-ch, changing to yarn B in the last yo of last st. Turn.

Row 3: 2 ch, *[dc (*UK tr*), SpDc (*UK SpTr*) in middle st of
skipped sts from two rows below, dc (*UK tr*)] in 1-ch sp,
1 ch, skip 3 sts, rep from * until 1 st rem, dc (*UK tr*) in top
of 2-ch. Turn.

Rep Row 3 until desired height, changing to the next
colour every two rows.

Fasten off and sew in ends.

Granny Ripple

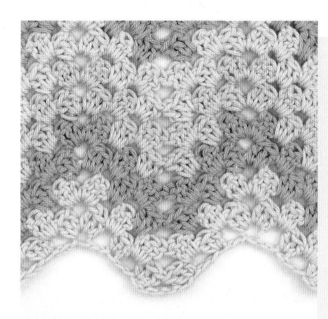

Skill level
Intermediate

Multiples
18 + 5

Stitches used
ch, dc (*UK tr*)

Pattern note
This sample is made with three colours changing every two rows; however, it can be made in any number of colours, which can change in any number of rows.

Colours
Sea Foam (A), Blush Pink (B), Vanilla Cream (C)

INSTRUCTIONS

Row 1: with yarn A 3 dc (*UK 3 tr*) in fifth ch from hook (skipped 4-ch counts as ch sp), [skip 2 ch, 3 dc (*UK 3 tr*) in next ch] twice, *skip 5 ch, [3 dc (*UK 3 tr*) in next ch, skip 2 ch] twice, [3 dc (*UK 3 tr*), 3 ch, 3 dc (*UK 3 tr*)] in next ch**, [skip 2 ch, 3 dc (*UK 3 tr*) in next ch] twice, rep from * until 12 ch rem, rep from * to ** across. Turn.

Row 2: 4 ch (counts as ch sp), 3 dc (*UK 3 tr*) in ch-sp, [3 dc (*UK 3 tr*) in sp between next set of 3-dc (*UK 3-tr*) from previous row] twice, *skip next sp between 3-dc (*UK 3-tr*) sets, [3 dc (*UK 3 tr*) in next sp] twice, [3 dc (*UK 3 tr*), 3 ch, 3 dc (*UK 3 tr*)] in ch sp, [3 dc (*UK 3 tr*) in next sp] twice, rep from * until four sets of 3-dc (*UK 3-tr*) rem, skip next sp between sets of 3-dc (*UK 3-tr*), [3 dc (*UK 3 tr*) in next sp] twice, [3 dc (*UK 3 tr*), 3 ch, 3 dc (*UK 3 tr*)] in last ch sp, changing to yarn B in last yo of final st. Turn.

Row 3: rep Row 2, omitting the colour change.

Row 4: rep Row 2, changing to yarn C in last yo of final st. Turn.

Rep Row 2 until desired height, changing to the next colour every two rows.

Fasten off and sew in ends.

Larksfoot

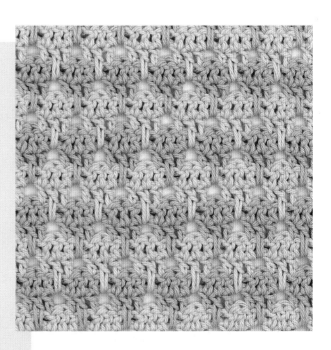

Skill level
Intermediate

Multiples
4 + 3

Stitches used
ch, dc (*UK tr*), SpDc (*UK SpTr*) –
see 'Special stitch' below

Special stitch
**SpDc (*UK SpTr*) = Spike Double Crochet
(*UK Spike Treble Crochet*):** dc (*UK tr*) into
indicated ch-sp from two rows below

Colours
Vanilla Cream (A), Pistachio Green (B)

INSTRUCTIONS

Row 1: with yarn A dc (*UK tr*) in fourth ch from hook
(skipped 3-ch count as dc (*UK tr*)), dc (*UK tr*) in next 2 ch,
*1 ch, skip a ch, dc (*UK tr*) in next 3 ch, rep from * until
1 ch rem, dc (*UK tr*) in last ch. Turn.

Row 2: 3 ch (counts as dc (*UK tr*) here and throughout),
dc (*UK tr*) in next 3 sts, *1 ch, skip ch sp, dc (*UK tr*) in next
3 sts, rep from * until 1 st rem, dc (*UK tr*) in top of 3-ch,
changing to yarn B in last yo of st. Turn.

Row 3: 3 ch, dc (*UK tr*) in next st, *1 ch, skip next st,
dc (*UK tr*) in next st, SpDc (*UK SpTr*), dc (*UK tr*) in next st,
rep from *until 3 sts rem, 1 ch, skip next st, dc (*UK tr*) in
last 2 sts. Turn.

Row 4: 3 ch, dc (*UK tr*) in next st, 1 ch, skip ch sp,
*dc (*UK tr*) in next 3 sts, 1 ch, skip ch sp, rep from * until
2 sts rem, dc (*UK tr*) in last 2 sts, changing to yarn A in
last yo of last st. Turn.

Row 5: 3 ch, dc (*UK tr*) in next st, SpDc (*UK SpTr*),
dc (*UK tr*) in next st, *1 ch, skip next st, dc (*UK tr*) in
next st, SpDc (*UK Tr*), dc (*UK tr*) in next st, rep from *
across until 1 st rem, dc (*UK tr*) in top of 3-ch. Turn.

Row 6: 3 ch, dc (*UK tr*) in next 3 sts, *1 ch, skip ch sp,
dc (*UK tr*) in next 3 sts, rep from * until 1 st rem, dc (*UK tr*)
in top of beginning 3-ch, changing to yarn B in the last
yo of the st. Turn.

Rep Rows 3–6 until desired height.

Fasten off and sew in ends.

Solomon's Knot

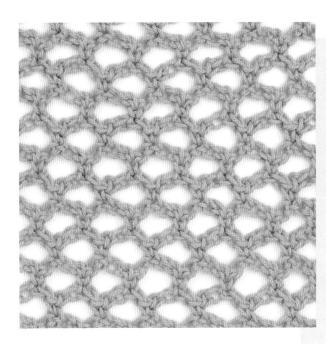

Skill level
Advanced

Multiples
4 + 2

Stitches used
ch, sc (*UK dc*), SK – see 'Special stitch' below, tr (*UK dtr*)

Special stitch
SK = Solomon's Knot: pull up a loop to around ½in (12mm) tall, 1 ch, insert hook between the first and second loop of the 3 loops below hook and complete a sc (*UK dc*) (known as a closing sc (*UK closing dc*))

Colour
Blush Pink

INSTRUCTIONS

Row 1: sc (*UK dc*) in second ch from hook (skipped ch does not count as a st), *2 SK, skip 3 ch, sc (*UK dc*) in next ch, rep from * across. Turn.

Row 2: 5 ch, SK, skip first sc (*UK dc*) and SK, *sc (*UK dc*) in next closing sc (*UK closing dc*), 2 SK, skip [SK, sc (*UK dc*), SK], rep from * until 1 closing sc (*UK closing dc*) rem, sc (*UK dc*) in closing sc (*UK closing dc*), SK, tr (*UK dtr*) in last sc (*UK dc*). Turn.

Row 3: 1 ch, sc (*UK dc*) in first closing sc (*UK closing dc*), *2 SK, skip [SK, sc (*UK dc*), SK], sc (*UK dc*) in next closing sc (*UK closing dc*), rep from * across working final sc (*UK dc*) in top of 5-ch. Turn.

Rep Rows 2 and 3 until desired height.

Final Row: 5 ch, *sc (*UK dc*) in closing sc (*UK closing dc*), 3 ch, rep from * across, 2 ch (so that you are ending with a 5-ch), sl st into starting 1-ch of previous row.

Fasten off and sew in ends.

Cobble

Skill level
Beginner

Multiples
2 + 2

Stitches used
ch, sc (*UK dc*), tr (*UK dtr*)

Colour
Pistachio Green

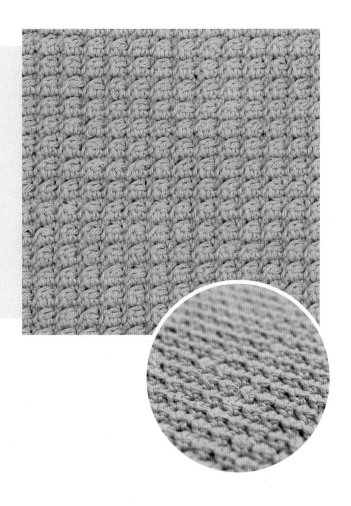

INSTRUCTIONS

Row 1: sc (*UK dc*) into second ch from hook (skipped ch does not count as st), sc (*UK dc*) in each ch across. Turn.
Row 2: 1 ch (does not count as a st here or throughout), sc (*UK dc*) in first st, *tr (*UK dtr*) in next st, sc (*UK dc*) in next st, rep from * across. Turn.
Row 3: 1 ch, sc (*UK dc*) in each st across. Turn.
Rep Rows 2 and 3 until desired height, finishing on a Row 2.
Fasten off and sew in ends.

Floret

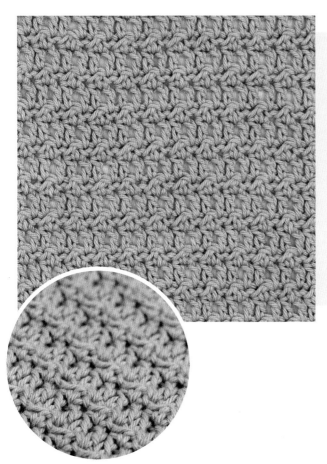

Skill level
Beginner

Multiples
2 + 2

Stitches used
ch, dc (*UK tr*), sl st

Colour
Stormy Grey

INSTRUCTIONS

Row 1: dc (*UK tr*) in fourth ch from hook (skipped 3-ch counts as st), dc (*UK tr*) in each ch across. Turn.

Row 2: 1 ch (does not count as st), *dc (*UK tr*) in next st, sl st in next st, rep from * to end. Turn.

Row 3: 3 ch (counts as dc (*UK tr*)), dc (*UK tr*) in each st across. Turn.

Rep Rows 2 and 3 until desired height.

Fasten off and sew in ends.

Rice

Skill level
Beginner

Multiples
2 + 3

Stitches used
ch, dc (*UK tr*), hdc (*UK htr*)

Pattern note
Refer to pages 172 and 173 for more information on FP and BP stitches.

Colour
Sea Foam

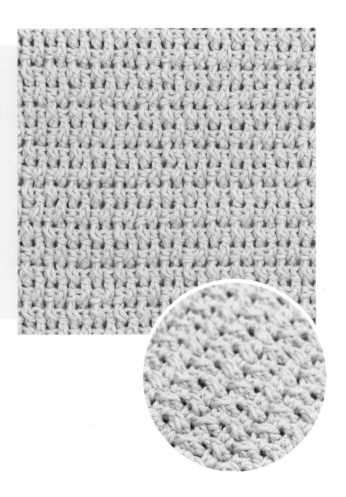

INSTRUCTIONS

Row 1: dc (*UK tr*) in third ch from the hook (skipped 2-ch counts as st), dc (*UK tr*) in each ch across. Turn.

Row 2: 1 ch (does not count as a st here and throughout), hdc (*UK htr*) in first st, *FPdc (*UK FPtr*) around next st, BPdc (*UK BPtr*) around next st, rep from * until 2 sts rem, FPdc (*UK FPtr*), hdc (*UK htr*) in last st. Turn.

Rep Row 2 until desired height.

Fasten off and sew in ends.

Even Berry

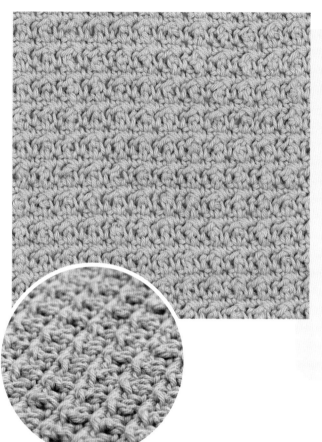

Skill level
Beginner

Multiples
2 + 2

Stitches used
ch, sc (*UK dc*), sl st, Berry – see 'Special stitch' below

Special stitch
Berry = Berry Stitch: yo, insert hook into next st, yo and pull up a loop (3 loops on hook), yo, pull through 1 loop, yo, insert hook into same st, yo, pull through (5 loops on hook), yo and pull through rem 5 loops

Colour
Pistachio Green

INSTRUCTIONS

Row 1: sc (*UK dc*) in second ch from hook (skipped ch does not count as st), sc (*UK dc*) in each ch across. Turn.

Row 2: 1 ch (does not count as st here or throughout), sl st in first st, *Berry, sl st in next st, rep from * across. Turn.

Row 3: 1 ch, sc (*UK dc*) in first st, *sl st in next st, sc (*UK dc*) in next st, rep from * across. Turn.

Rep Rows 2 and 3 until desired height, finishing on a Row 2.

Fasten off and sew in ends.

Lace Cluster

Skill level
Beginner

Multiples
6 + 5

Stitches used
ch, dc (*UK tr*), hdccl (*UK htrcl*) –
see 'Special stitch' below

Special stitch
**hdccl (*UK htrcl*) = Half Double Crochet Cluster
(*UK Half Treble Cluster*):** [yo, insert hook into st,
yo, pull through] four times into next st, yo, pull
through all loops on the hook, 1 ch to secure cluster

Colour
Sea Foam

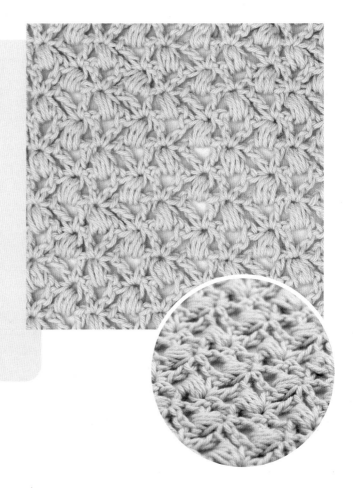

INSTRUCTIONS

Row 1: [dc (*UK tr*), 2 ch, dc (*UK tr*)] in fourth ch from
hook (skipped 3-ch counts as dc (*UK tr*)), skip 2 ch,
*hdccl (*UK htrcl*), skip 2 ch, [dc (*UK tr*), 2 ch, dc (*UK tr*)] in
next ch, rep from * until 1 ch rem, dc (*UK tr*) in last ch.
Turn.

Row 2: 3 ch, *hdccl (*UK htrcl*) into the ch sp from previous
row, [dc (*UK tr*), 2 ch, dc (*UK tr*)] into top of next hdccl
(*UK htrcl*) from previous row, rep from * until 1 ch sp rem,
hdccl (*UK htrcl*) in last ch sp, dc (*UK tr*) in top of 3-ch. Turn.

Row 3: 3 ch, *[dc (*UK tr*), 2 ch, dc (*UK tr*)] into top of next
hdccl (*UK htrcl*) from previous row, hdccl (*UK htrcl*) into
next ch sp from previous row, rep from * until
1 hdccl (*UK 1 htrcl*) rem, [dc (*UK tr*), 2 ch, dc (*UK tr*)] in last
hdccl (*UK htrcl*), dc (*UK tr*) in top of 3-ch. Turn.

Rep Rows 2 and 3 until desired height.

Fasten off and sew in ends.

Even Moss

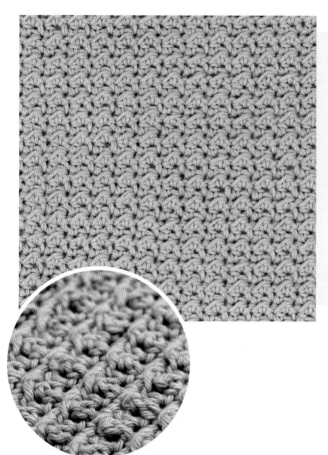

Skill level
Beginner

Multiples
2 + 2

Stitches used
ch, sl st, hdc (*UK htr*)

Colour
Pistachio Green

INSTRUCTIONS

Row 1: sl st in second ch from hook (skipped ch does not count as st), *hdc (*UK htr*) in next ch, sl st in next ch, rep from * across. Turn.

Row 2: 1 ch (does not count as st), *sl st in next st, hdc (*UK htr*) in next st, rep from * across until 1 st rem, sl st in last st. Turn.

Rep Row 2 until desired height.

Fasten off and sew in ends.

Knit

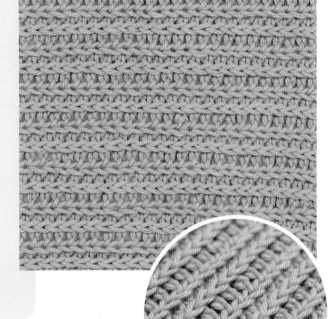

Skill level
Intermediate

Multiples
1 + 2

Stitches used
ch, hdc (*UK htr*)

Pattern notes
- Refer to page 172 for more information on BLO.
- If you need to remind yourself of where the third loop is in your half double crochet (*UK half treble crochet*) stitch, see page 34.

Colour
Blush Pink

INSTRUCTIONS

Row 1 (WS): hdc (*UK htr*) in third ch from hook (missed 2-ch counts as st), hdc (*UK htr*) in each ch across. Turn.

Row 2 (RS): 2 ch (does not count as st here or throughout), [hdc (*UK htr*) in third loop] across to last st, hdc (*UK htr*) in last st. Turn.

Row 3: 2 ch, BLOhdc (*UK BLOhtr*) in each st across to last st, hdc (*UK htr*) in last st. Turn.

Repeat Rows 2 and 3 to desired height.

Fasten off and sew in ends.

Almond Ridges

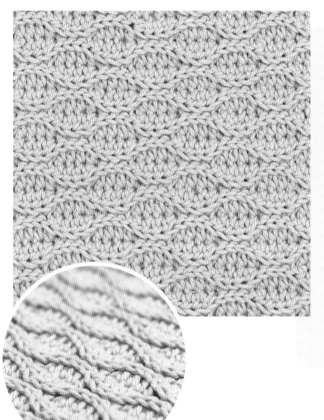

Skill level
Intermediate

Multiples
8 + 5

Stitches used
ch, sl st, hdc (*UK htr*)

Pattern note
Refer to page 172 for more information on BLO.

Colour
Vanilla Cream

INSTRUCTIONS

Row 1 (RS): sl st in second ch from hook (skipped ch does not count as st), sl st in next 3 ch, *hdc (*UK htr*) in next 4 ch, sl st in next 4 ch, rep from * across. Turn.

Rows 2 and 3 (WS): 1 ch (does not count as st here or throughout), *BLOhdc (*UK BLOhtr*) in next 4 sts, BLOsl st in next 4 sl st, rep from * until 4 sts rem, BLOhdc (*UK BLOhtr*) in last 4 sts. Turn.

Rows 4 and 5 (RS): 1 ch, *BLOsl st in next 4 sl st, BLOhdc (*UK BLOhtr*) in next 4 sts, rep from * until 4 sts rem, BLOsl st in last 4 sl st. Turn.

Rep Rows 2–5 until desired height.

Final Row (WS): 1 ch, *BLOhdc (*UK BLOhtr*) in next 4 sts, BLOsl st in next 4 sl st, rep from * until 4 sts rem, BLOhdc (*UK BLOhtr*) in last 4 sts.

Fasten off and sew in ends.

Alpine

Skill level
Intermediate

Multiples
2 + 1

Stitches used
ch, sc (*UK dc*), dc (*UK tr*)

Pattern notes
- Refer to page 173 for more information on FP stitches.
- When working a front post double crochet (*UK front post treble*), you will skip the stitch just worked over on the current row.

Colour
Blush pink

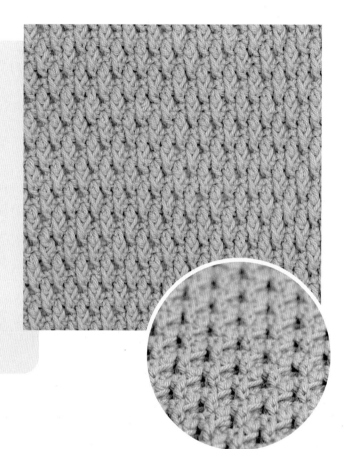

INSTRUCTIONS

Row 1 (WS): sc (*UK dc*) in second ch from hook (skipped ch does not count as st), sc (*UK dc*) in each ch across. Turn.

Row 2 (RS): 2 ch (counts as dc (*UK tr*) here and throughout), dc (*UK tr*) in each st across. Turn.

Row 3: 1 ch (does not count as st here and throughout), sc (*UK dc*) in each st across. Turn.

Row 4: 2 ch, *FPdc (*UK FPtr*) around next st two rows below, dc (*UK tr*) in next st, rep from * to last st, dc (*UK tr*) in last st. Turn.

Row 5: 1 ch, sc (*UK dc*) in each st across. Turn.

Row 6: 2 ch, *dc (*UK tr*) in next st, FPdc (*UK FPtr*) around next st two rows below, rep from * to last st, dc (*UK tr*) in last st. Turn.

Rep Rows 3–6 until desired height.

Final Row: 1 ch, sc (*UK dc*) in each st across. Turn.

Fasten off and sew in ends.

Basketweave

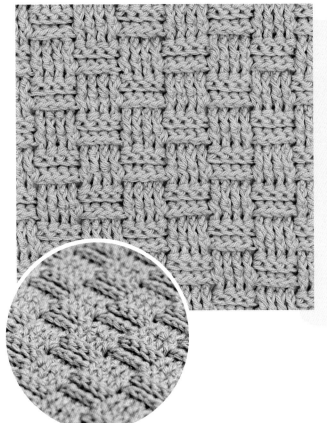

Skill level
Intermediate

Multiples
8 + 7

Stitches used
ch, dc (*UK tr*), hdc (*UK htr*)

Pattern note
Refer to pages 173 and 173 for more information on BP and FP stitches.

Colour
Stormy Grey

INSTRUCTIONS

Row 1: dc (*UK tr*) into third ch from hook (skipped 2-ch counts as a st), dc (*UK tr*) in each ch across. Turn.

Row 2: 2 ch (counts as hdc (*UK htr*) here and throughout), *FPdc (*UK FPtr*) around next 4 sts, BPdc (*UK BPtr*) around next 4 sts, rep from * until 5 sts rem, FPdc (*UK FPtr*) around next 4 sts, hdc (*UK htr*) in top of 2-ch. Turn.

Row 3: 2 ch, *BPdc (*UK BPtr*) around next 4 sts, FPdc (*UK FPtr*) around next 4 sts, rep from * until 5 sts rem, BPdc (*UK BPtr*) around next 4 sts, hdc (*UK htr*) in top of 2-ch. Turn.

Row 4: 2 ch, *BPdc (*UK BPtr*) around next 4 sts, FPdc (*UK FPtr*) around next 4 sts, rep from * until 5 sts rem, BPdc (*UK BPtr*) around next 4 sts, hdc (*UK htr*) in top of 2-ch. Turn.

Row 5: 2 ch, *FPdc (*UK FPtr*) around next 4 sts, BPdc (*UK BPtr*) around next 4 sts, rep from * until 5 sts rem, FPdc (*UK FPtr*) around next 4 sts, hdc (*UK htr*) in top of 2-ch. Turn.

Rep Rows 2–5 until desired height.

Fasten off and sew in ends.

Popcorn

Skill level
Intermediate

Multiples
2 + 2

Stitches used
ch, sc (*UK dc*), PSt – see 'Special stitch' below

Special stitch
PSt = Popcorn Stitch: work 5 dc (*UK 5 tr*) into st, loosen the loop on your hook then carefully remove hook, insert hook into top of first dc (*UK tr*) from back to front, insert hook back into the working loop (the one from which you removed your hook), pull the loop through the dc (*UK tr*) st

Pattern note
Each of the Popcorn stitches will be worked from the wrong side of the work. This means that your stitches will 'pop' away from you.

Colour
Sea Foam

INSTRUCTIONS

Row 1 (WS): sc (*UK dc*) in second ch from hook (skipped ch does not count as st), *PSt in next ch, sc (*UK dc*) in next ch, rep from * across. Turn.

Row 2 (RS): 1 ch (does not count as st here or throughout), sc (*UK dc*) in each st across. Turn.

Row 3: 1 ch, sc (*UK dc*) in first st, *PSt in next st, sc (*UK dc*) in next st, rep from * across. Turn.

Rep Rows 2 and 3 until desired height.

Fasten off and sew in ends.

Puff

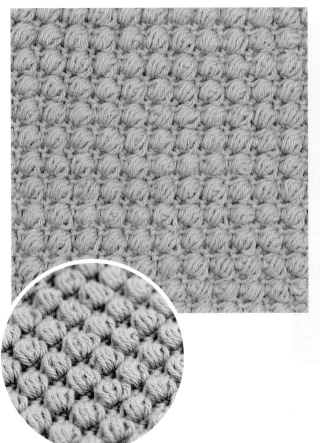

Skill level
Intermediate

Multiples
2 + 2

Stitches used
ch, sc (*UK dc*), PS – see 'Special stitch' below

Special stitch
PS = Puff Stitch: insert hook into st, yo, pull through st and bring up to height of loop, [yo, insert hook into same st, yo and pull through st] twice (6 loops on hook), yo and pull through rem 6 loops on hook, 1 ch to secure the st

Colour
Blush Pink

INSTRUCTIONS

Row 1 (RS): sc (*UK dc*) in second ch from hook (skipped chain does not count as st), sc (*UK dc*) in each ch across. Turn.

Row 2 (WS): 1 ch (does not count as st here or throughout), sc (*UK dc*) in first st, *PS in next st, sc (*UK dc*) in next st, rep from * across. Turn.

Row 3: 1 ch, sc (*UK dc*) in each st across. Turn.

Rep Rows 2 and 3 until desired height.

Final Row: rep Row 2.

Fasten off and sew in ends.

Zigzag Puff

Skill level
Intermediate

Multiples
2 + 1

Stitches used
ch, sc (*UK dc*), PS – see 'Special stitch' below, hdc (*UK htr*)

Special stitch
PS = Puff Stitch: insert hook into st, yo, pull through st and bring up to height of loop, [yo, insert hook into same st, yo and pull through st] twice (6 loops on hook), yo and pull through rem 6 loops on hook, 1 ch to secure st

Colour
Vanilla Cream

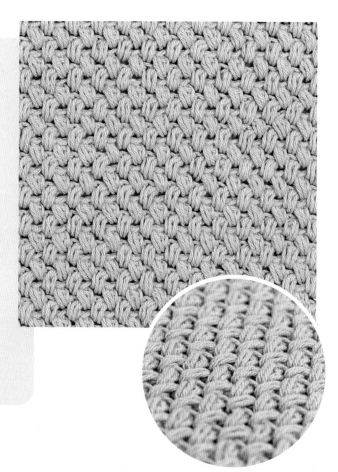

INSTRUCTIONS

Row 1: sc (*UK dc*) in second ch from hook (skipped ch does not count as st), sc (*UK dc*) in each ch across. Turn.

Row 2: 2 ch (counts as hdc (*UK htr*) here and throughout), *skip next st, PS, rep from * across until 2 sts rem, skip next st, hdc (*UK htr*) in last st of row. Turn.

Row 3: 2 ch, skip sp before first PS, work PS in each sp between PSs across, work PS in sp after last PS, work hdc (*UK htr*) in top of 2-ch. Turn.

Rep Row 3 until desired height.

Fasten off and sew in ends.

Harvest

Skill level
Intermediate

Multiples
7 + 3

Stitches used
ch, sc (*UK dc*), dc (*UK tr*),
DPS – see 'Special stitch' below

Special stitch
DPS = Double Puff Stitch: yo, insert hook into st,
yo, pull through st and bring up to height of loop,
[yo, insert hook into same st, yo and pull through st]
four times (11 loops on hook), yo, pull through 10 loops
on hook, yo, pull through rem loops on hook, 1 ch to
secure st

Colour
Pistachio Green

INSTRUCTIONS

Row 1 (RS): sc (*UK dc*) in second ch from the hook
(skipped ch does not count as st), sc (*UK dc*) in each ch
across. Turn.

Row 2 (WS): 3 ch (counts as dc (*UK tr*) here and
throughout), dc (*UK tr*) in next st, *skip 2 sts, [DPS, 2 ch,
DPS] in next st, skip 2 sts, dc (*UK tr*) in next 2 sts, rep from
* across. Turn.

Row 3: 3 ch, dc (*UK tr*) in next st, *skip DPS, [DPS, 2 ch,
DPS] in ch sp, skip DPS, dc (*UK tr*) in next 2 sts, rep from *
across. Turn.

Rep Row 3 until desired height.

Fasten off and sew in ends.

Waffle

Skill level
Intermediate

Multiples
3 + 2

Stitches used
ch, dc (*UK tr*)

Pattern note
Refer to page 173 for more information on FP stitches.

Colour
Blush Pink

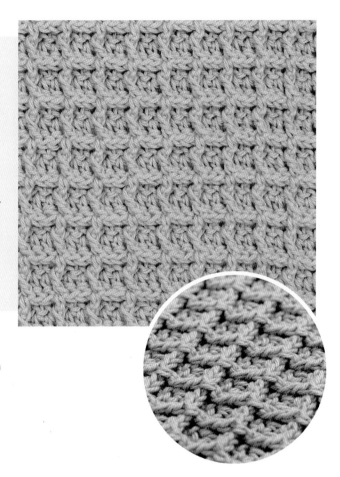

INSTRUCTIONS

Row 1 (WS): dc (*UK tr*) in third ch from hook (skipped 2-ch does not count as st), dc (*UK tr*) in each ch across. Turn.

Row 2 (RS): 3 ch (counts as dc (*UK tr*) here and throughout), *FPdc (*UK FPtr*) around next st, dc (*UK tr*) into next 2 sts, rep from * until 2 sts rem, FPdc (*UK FPtr*) around next st, dc (*UK tr*) in last st. Turn.

Row 3: 3 ch, dc (*UK tr*) in next st, *FPdc (*UK FPtr*) around next 2 sts, dc (*UK tr*) in next st, rep from * until 1 st rem, dc (*UK tr*) in last st. Turn.

Rep Rows 2 and 3 until desired height.

Final Row: 3 ch, dc (*UK tr*) in each st across.

Fasten off and sew in ends.

Double Waffle

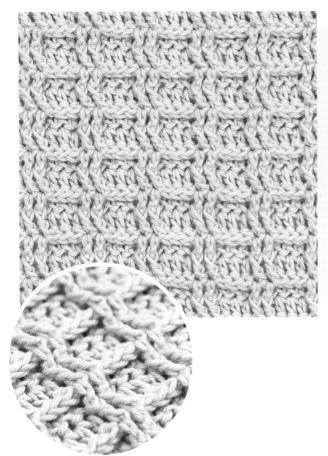

Skill level
Intermediate

Multiples
5 + 2

Stitches used
ch, dc (*UK tr*)

Pattern note
Refer to page 173 for more information on FP stitches.

Colour
Sea Foam

INSTRUCTIONS

Row 1 (RS): dc (*UK tr*) in third ch from hook (skipped 2-ch does not count as st), dc (*UK tr*) in each ch across. Turn.

Row 2 (WS): 2 ch (does not count as st here or throughout), dc (*UK tr*) in first st, FPdc (*UK FPtr*) around next 3 sts, *dc (*UK tr*) in next 2 sts, FPdc (*UK FPtr*) in next 3 sts, rep from * until 1 st rem, dc (*UK tr*) in last st. Turn.

Row 3: 2 ch, dc (*UK tr*) in first st and in next 3 sts, *FPdc (*UK FPtr*) around next 2 sts, dc (*UK tr*) in next 3 sts, rep from * across until 1 st rem, dc (*UK tr*) in last st. Turn.

Rep Rows 2 and 3 until desired height.

Fasten off and sew in ends.

Bobble

Skill level
Intermediate

Multiples
2 + 2

Stitches used
ch, sc (*UK dc*), Bobble – see 'Special stitch' below

Special stitch
Bobble = Bobble Stitch: yo, insert hook into next st, yoand pull up a loop, yo and pull through 2 loops on the hook (2 loops on hook), [yo, insert hook into same st, yo and pull up a loop, yo and pull through 2 loops] four times (6 loops on hook), yo and pull though rem 6 loops on hook, 1 ch to secure

Colour
Pistachio

INSTRUCTIONS

Row 1 (RS): sc (*UK dc*) in second ch from hook (skipped ch does not count as st), sc (*UK dc*) in each ch across. Turn.

Row 2 (WS): 1 ch (does not count as st here or throughout), *Bobble in next st, sc (*UK dc*) in next st, rep from * until 1 st rem, Bobble in last st. Turn.

Row 3: 1 ch, sc (*UK dc*) in each st across. Turn.

Rep Rows 2 and 3 until desired height.

Fasten off and sew in ends.

Feather

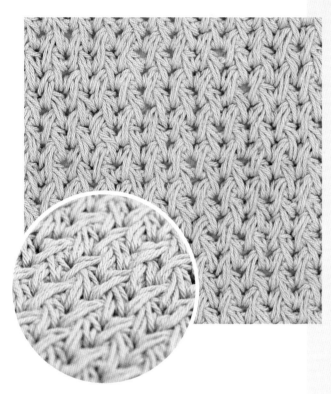

INSTRUCTIONS

Foundation Row: using Foundation Half Double Crochet (*UK Foundation Half Treble*) work your desired number of sts in multiples of 2 + 1.

Row 1: 1 ch (does not count as st here or throughout), hdc (*UK htr*) in first st, *1 ch, skip next st, hdc (*UK htr*) in next st, rep from * across. Turn.

Row 2: 1 ch, hdc (*UK htr*) in first st, 1 ch, work BFS, 1 ch, *FeS, 1 ch, rep from * until 1 st rem, hdc (*UK htr*) in last st. Turn.

Rep Row 2 until desired height.

Final Row: 1 ch, hdc (*UK htr*) in first st, *hdc (*UK htr*) in next ch sp, hdc (*UK htr*) in FeS, rep from * across, hdc (*UK htr*) in last st.

Fasten off and sew in ends.

Skill level
Intermediate

Multiples
2 + 1

Stitches used
Foundation Half Double Crochet (*UK Foundation Half Treble Crochet*) – see 'Special stitches' below, ch, hdc (*UK htr*), BFS – see 'Special stitches' below, FeS – see 'Special stitches' below

Special stitches
Foundation Half Double Crochet (*UK Foundation Half Treble*): 2 ch, yo and insert hook into second ch from hook, yo and pull up a loop, 1 ch (this creates a 'ch'), yo and pull through all 3 loops on hook (this creates 1 hdc (*UK 1 htr*)), *yo and insert hook into 'ch' just made, yo and pull up a loop, 1 ch, yo and pull though rem 3 loops on hook, rep from * for indicated number of sts

BFS = Beginning Feather Stitch: yo, insert hook into first ch sp, yo and pull up a loop in line with loops on the hook (3 loops on hook), yo, insert hook into 1-ch sp or skipped st two rows below, yo and pull up a loop in line with loops on the hook (5 loops on hook), yo, insert hook in next 1-ch sp, yo and pull up a loop in line with loops on the hook, yo and pull through rem 7 loops on the hook

FeS = Feather Stitch: yo, insert hook into same 1-ch sp as last part of BFS or FeS, yo and pull up a loop in line with loops on hook (3 loops on hook), yo, insert hook into 1-ch sp or skipped st two rows below, yo and pull up a loop in line with loops on hook (5 loops on hook), yo, insert hook in next 1-ch sp, yo and pull up a loop in line with loops on the hook, yo and pull through rem 7 loops on the hook

Pattern note
When working Row 2 for the first time, the central part of the BFS or FeS should be worked into the skipped stitch from Row 1. On subsequent reps of Row 2, you will work into the 1-ch sp from two rows below.

Colour
Vanilla Cream

Corded Ridge

Skill level
Intermediate

Multiples
1 + 1

Stitches used
ch, dc (*UK tr*), Rsc (*UK Rdc*) – see 'Special stitch' below

Special stitch
**Rsc (*UK Rdc*) = Reverse Single Crochet
(*UK Reverse Double Crochet*):** without turning
the work, insert hook into previous st from the
last row, yo and pull up a loop, yo and pull
through both loops

Pattern note
At the end of each row, you will NOT turn your work.
For every row, you will be working with the right side
facing you.

Colour
Blush Pink

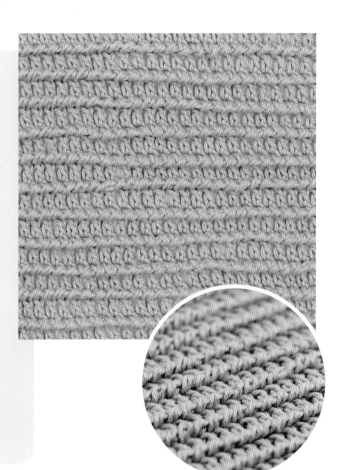

INSTRUCTIONS

Row 1 (RS): dc (*UK tr*) in third ch from hook (skipped
2-ch counts as st), dc (*UK tr*) in each ch across.
Do not turn.

Row 2 (RS): 1 ch (does not count as st), working into
the front loop only, Rsc (*UK Rdc*) in each st across.
Do not turn.

Row 3: 3 ch (counts as dc (*UK tr*)), working into the
unworked loop of st from two rows below, dc (*UK tr*)
in each st across. Do not turn.

Rep Rows 2 and 3 until desired height.

Fasten off and sew in ends.

Mini Basketweave

Skill level
Intermediate

Multiples
4 + 2

Stitches used
ch, dc (*UK tr*), hdc (*UK htr*)

Pattern note
Refer to pages 172 and 173 for more information on BP and FP stitches.

Colour
Sea Foam

INSTRUCTIONS

Row 1: dc (*UK tr*) in fourth ch from hook (skipped 3-ch counts as st), dc (*UK tr*) in each ch across. Turn.

Row 2: 2 ch (counts as hdc (*UK htr*) here and throughout), *BPdc (*UK BPtr*) around next 2 sts, FPdc (*UK FPtr*) around next 2 sts, rep from * across until 3 sts rem, BPdc (*UK BPtr*) around next 2 sts, hdc (*UK htr*) in top of turning ch. Turn.

Row 3: 2 ch, *FPdc (*UK FPtr*) around next 2 sts, BPdc (*UK BPtr*) around next 2 sts, rep from * until 3 sts rem, FPdc (*UK FPtr*) around next 2 sts, hdc (*UK htr*) in top of 2-ch. Turn.

Row 4: rep Row 3.

Row 5: rep Row 2.

Rep Rows 2–5 until desired height.

Fasten off and sew in ends.

Loop

Skill level
Intermediate

Multiples
1 + 1

Stitches used
ch, sc (*UK dc*), LS – see 'Special stitch' below

Special stitch
LS = Loop Stitch: insert hook into st, wrap yarn around index finger and keep finger at desired distance from crochet (this will determine size of loop), bring hook over the top strand of loop around finger then catch the bottom strand of the loop to yo, pull through (2 loops on hook), carefully slip loop off finger and pinch it with middle finger to hold it in place, pick up working yarn with hook (being careful not to pull on the loop made), pull through both loops on hook to complete loop

Colour
Vanilla Cream

INSTRUCTIONS

Row 1 (RS): sc (*UK dc*) in second ch from hook (skipped ch does not count as st), sc (*UK dc*) in each ch across. Turn.

Row 2 (WS): 1 ch (does not count as st here or throughout), LS in each st across. Turn.

Row 3: 1 ch, sc (*UK dc*) in each st across. Turn.

Rep Rows 2 and 3 until desired height, finishing on a Row 3.

Fasten off and sew in ends.

Diamond Waffle

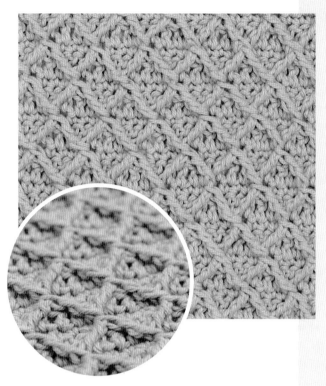

Skill level
Intermediate

Multiples
4 + 2

Stitches used
ch, sc (*UK dc*), dc (*UK tr*),
Diamond St – see 'Special stitch' below

Special stitch
Diamond St = Diamond Stitch: working around
same st as the previous FPtr (*UK FPdtr*) or
FPtr2tog (*UK FPdtr2tog*), work FPtr (*UK FPdtr*)
but leave last 2 loops on hook, skip next 3 sts
from two rows below, begin FPtr (*UK FPdtr*)
around next FPtr (*UK FPdtr*) until there are 3 loops
on hook, yo and pull through rem 3 loops

Pattern notes
– Refer to page 173 for more information on
  FP stitches.
– You will actually be working FPtr2tog (*UK FPdtr2tog*)
  in this pattern, but for ease it'll be referred to as
  Diamond St.

Colour
Blush Pink

INSTRUCTIONS

Row 1 (RS): sc (*UK dc*) in second ch from hook
(skipped ch does not count as st), sc (*UK dc*) in each
ch across. Turn.

Row 2 (WS): 2 ch (does not count as a st here or
throughout), dc (*UK tr*) in first st and across. Turn.

Row 3: 1 ch (does not count as a st here or throughout),
FPtr (*UK FPdtr*) around third sc (*UK dc*) of Row 1, skip st
covered by the FPtr (*UK FPdtr*) and sc (*UK dc*) in next
3 sts, *Diamond St, skip st covered by Diamond st,
sc (*UK dc*) into next 3 sts, rep from * until 1 st rem,
FPtr (*UK FPdtr*) around same post as previous
FPtr (*UK FPdtr*) leaving 2 loops on hook, sc (*UK dc*) in
last st, pulling through all 3 loops on the hook. Turn.

Row 4: 2 ch, dc (*UK tr*) in each st across. Turn.

Row 5: 1 ch, sc (*UK dc*) into first 2 sts, *Diamond St
working around the FPtr (*UK FPdtr*) and Diamond St
from two rows below, sc (*UK dc*) into the next 3 sts,
rep from * until 2 sts rem, sc (*UK dc*) in last 2 sts. Turn.

Row 6: 2 ch, dc (*UK tr*) in each st across. Turn.

Row 7: 1 ch, FPtr (*UK FPdtr*) around top of Diamond St
from Row 5, skip st covered by FPtr (*UK FPdtr*), sc (*UK dc*)
in next 3 sts, *Diamond St, sc (*UK dc*) into next 3 sts,
rep from * until 1 st rem, FPtr (*UK FPdtr*) around same
post as previous FPtr (*UK FPdtr*) leaving 2 loops on hook,
sc (*UK dc*) in last st, pulling through all 3 loops on the
hook. Turn.

Rep Rows 4–7 until desired height.

Fasten off and sew in ends.

Bar

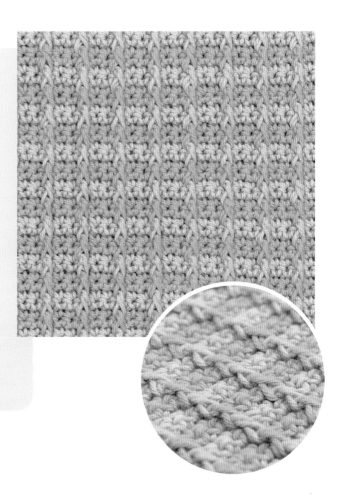

Skill level
Intermediate

Multiples
3 + 3

Stitches used
ch, sc (*UK dc*), dc (*UK tr*)

Pattern note
- Refer to page 172 for more information on BLO.
- Refer to page 173 for more information on FP stitches.
- When changing colours, you do not need to fasten off the yarn; instead carry the unused yarn up the edge of the work.

Colours
Vanilla Cream (A), Blush Pink (B)

INSTRUCTIONS

Row 1 (RS): with yarn A sc (*UK dc*) in second ch from hook (skipped ch does not count as st), sc (*UK dc*) in each ch across. Turn.

Row 2 (WS): 1 ch (does not count as st here or throughout), sc (*UK dc*) in each st across. Turn.

Row 3: 1 ch, sc (*UK dc*) in first 2 sts, FPdc (*UK FPtr*) around next st two rows below, *sc (*UK dc*) in next 2 sts, FPdc (*UK FPtr*) around next st two rows below, rep from * until 2 sts rem, sc (*UK dc*) in last 2 sts changing to yarn B in last yo of last st. Turn.

Row 4: 1 ch, sc (*UK dc*) in first st and each st across. Turn.

Row 5: 1 ch, sc (*UK dc*) in first 2 sts, FPdc (*UK FPtr*) around FPdc (*UK FPtr*) from two rows below, *sc (*UK dc*) in next 2 sts, FPdc (*UK FPtr*) around FPdc (*UK FPtr*) from two rows below, rep from * until 2 sts rem, sc (*UK dc*) in last 2 sts changing to yarn A in last yo of last st. Turn.

Row 6: 1 ch, sc (*UK dc*) in each st across. Turn.

Row 7: 1 ch, sc (*UK dc*) in first 2 sts, FPdc (*UK FPtr*) around FPdc (*UK FPtr*) from two rows below, *sc (*UK dc*) in next 2 sts, FPdc (*UK FPtr*) around FPdc (*UK FPtr*) from two rows below, rep from * until 2 sts rem, sc (*UK dc*) in last 2 sts changing to yarn B in the last yo of last st. Turn.

Rep Rows 4–7 until desired height, omitting colour change on final row.

Fasten off and sew in ends.

Royal Ridge

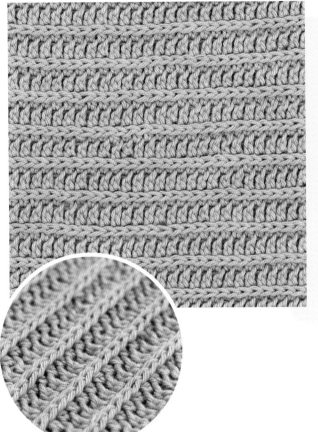

Skill level
Intermediate

Multiples
1 + 1

Stitches used
ch, sc (*UK dc*), hdc (*UK htr*)

Pattern note
If you need to remind yourself of where the third loop is in your half double crochet (*UK half treble crochet*) stitch, see page 34.

Colour
Stormy Grey

INSTRUCTIONS

Row 1 (RS): sc (*UK dc*) in second ch from hook (skipped ch does not count as st), sc (*UK dc*) in each ch across. Turn.

Row 2 (WS): 1 ch (does not count as st here or throughout), hdc (*UK htr*) in each st across. Turn.

Rows 3: 1 ch, hdc (*UK htr*) in third loop across to last st, hdc (*UK htr*) in last st. Turn.

Rep Row 3 until desired height.

Fasten off and sew in ends.

Arrow

Skill level
Advanced

Multiples
4 + 4

Stitches used
ch, sc (*UK dc*), dc (*UK tr*), FAS – see 'Special stitches' below, AS – see 'Special stitches' below, BAS – see 'Special stitches' below

Special stitches
AS = Arrow Stitch: yo twice, insert hook into st beneath previous ch sp two rows down from front to back, yo and pull through (4 loops on hook), yo and pull through 2 loops (3 loops on hook), yo and pull through 2 loops (2 loops on hook), yo twice, insert hook under next 1-ch sp two rows down from front to back, yo over and pull through (5 loops on hook), yo over and pull through 2 loops (4 loops on hook), yo and pull through 2 loops (3 loops on hook), yo and pull through rem 3 loops on the hook

FAS = Forward Arrow Stitch: yo over twice, insert hook into st beneath previous ch sp two rows down from front to back, yo and pull through (4 loops on hook), yo over and pull through 2 loops (3 loops on hook), yo and pull through 2 loops (2 loops on hook), yo and pull through rem 2 loops on the hook

BAS = Backward Arrow Stitch: yo over twice, insert hook into st beneath previous ch sp two rows down from front to back, yo and pull through (4 loops on hook), yo and pull through 2 loops (3 loops on hook), yo over and pull through 2 loops (2 loops on hook), yo and pull through rem 2 loops on the hook

Colour
Pistachio Green

INSTRUCTIONS

Row 1: sc (*UK dc*) in second ch from hook (skipped ch does not count as st), sc (*UK dc*) in next 2 ch, *1 ch, skip next ch, sc (*UK dc*) in next 3 ch, rep from * across. Turn.

Row 2: 3 ch (counts as dc (*UK tr*)), dc (*UK tr*) in next 2 sts, *dc (*UK tr*) in ch sp, dc (*UK tr*) in next 3 sts, rep from * across. Turn.

Row 3: 1 ch (does not count as a st), sc (*UK dc*) in first st, FAS, skip 1 st (the st sitting behind FAS just worked), sc (*UK dc*) in next st, 1 ch, skip 1 st, *sc (*UK dc*) in next st, AS, skip 1 st (the st sitting behind AS just worked), sc (*UK dc*) in next st, 1 ch, skip 1 st, rep from * until 3 sts rem, sc (*UK dc*) in next st, BAS, skip 1 st (the st sitting behind BAS just worked), sc (*UK dc*) in top of 3-ch. Turn.

Rep Rows 2 and 3 until desired height.

Fasten off and sew in ends.

Crocodile

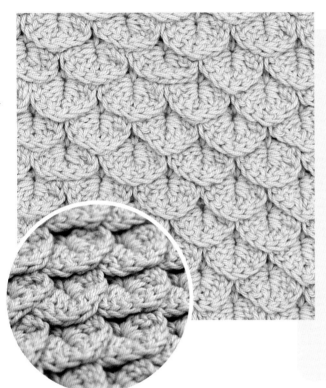

Skill level
Advanced

Multiples
6 + 3

Stitches used
ch, dc (*UK tr*), sl st, ScSt – see 'Special stitch' below

Special stitch
ScSt = Scale Stitch: work 5 dc (*UK 5 tr*) around post of the first dc (*UK tr*) of pair of dcs (*UK trs*) in previous row, rotate piece so it's upside down, work 5 dc (*UK 5 tr*) around post of second dc (*UK tr*) of pair of dcs (*UK trs*). One scale made

Colour
Vanilla Cream

INSTRUCTIONS

Row 1 (WS): 2 dc (*UK 2 tr*) into sixth ch from hook (skipped 5-ch counts as dc (*UK tr*) and skipped 2 ch), *1 ch, skip 2 ch, dc (*UK tr*) in next st, 1 ch, skip 2 ch, 2 dc (*UK 2 tr*) in next st, rep from * until 3 ch rem, 1 ch, skip 2 ch, dc (*UK tr*) in last ch. Turn.

Row 2 (RS): 1 ch (counts as sl st), *work ScSt around next 2 sts, sl st in top of next dc (*UK tr*), rep from * across, working final sl st in top of 5-ch. Turn.

Row 3: 3 ch (counts as dc (*UK tr*)), dc (*UK tr*) in base of 3-ch, *1 ch, dc (*UK tr*) in centre of scale in previous row, 1 ch, work 2 dc (*UK 2 tr*) in sl st from previous row, rep from * across, working final 2 dc (*UK 2 tr*) in 1-ch from previous row. Turn.

Row 4: 1 ch (does not count as st), ScSt around first 2 sts, sl st in top of next dc (*UK tr*), *work ScSt around next 2 sts, sl st in top of next dc (*UK tr*), rep from * across, working last part of last scale around 3-ch from previous row and omitting final sl st after last scale. Turn.

Row 5: 1 ch, sl st in centre of first scale, 4 ch (counts as dc (*UK tr*) and 1 ch), *work 2 dc (*UK 2 tr*) in sl st from previous row, 1 ch, dc (*UK tr*) in centre of next scale, 1 ch, rep from * across, omitting final 1-ch. Turn.

Rep Rows 2–5 until desired height. Note: when rep Row 2, work final sl st in third of 4-ch.

Fasten off and sew in ends.

Celtic Weave

Skill level
Advanced

Multiples
4 + 4

Stitches used
ch, dc (*UK tr*), tr (*UK dtr*), hdc (*UK htr*)

Pattern note
Refer to pages 172 and 173 for more information on BP and FP stitches.

Colour
Stormy Grey

INSTRUCTIONS

Row 1 (WS): dc (*UK tr*) in third ch from hook (skipped 2-ch does not count as a st), dc (*UK tr*) in each st across. Turn.

Row 2 (RS): 2 ch (does not count as st here or throughout), dc (*UK tr*) in first st, *skip 2 sts, FPtr (*UK FPdtr*) around next 2 sts, FPtr (*UK FPdtr*) around first skipped st, FPtr (*UK FPdtr*) around second skipped st, rep from * until 1 st rem, dc (*UK tr*) in last st. Turn.

Row 3: 2 ch, dc (*UK tr*) in first st, BPtr (*UK BPdtr*) around next 2 sts, *skip 2 sts, BPtr (*UK BPdtr*) around next 2 sts, BPtr (*UK BPdtr*) around first skipped st, BPtr (*UK BPdtr*) around second skipped st, rep from * until 3 sts rem, BPtr (*UK BPdtr*) around next 2 sts, dc (*UK tr*) in last st. Turn.

Rep Rows 2 and 3 until desired height.

Final Row: 1 ch (does not count as a st), hdc (*UK htr*) in each st across.

Fasten off and sew in ends.

Jasmine

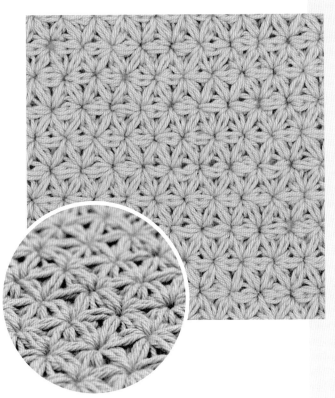

INSTRUCTIONS

Foundation row: 1 ch, fps in first ch. Continue to build row using fps, working into the top of the last puff st to your desired size. Turn.

Row 1: J-st across, working first puff st of J-st into the end of the final puff st of the foundation row and working last puff st of last J-st into outer edge of last puff st from previous row. Turn.

Row 2: work a fps into top of last st from previous row, J-st across working last puff st of last J-st into outer edge of last puff st from previous row. Turn.

Rep Row 2 until desired height.

Fasten off and sew in ends.

Skill level
Advanced

Multiples
1 + 1

Stitches used
ch, sc (*UK dc*), fps – see 'Special stitches' below, J-st – see 'Special stitches' below

Special stitches
fps = Foundation Puff Stitch: pull up a loop (around ¾in or 2cm tall), yo and insert hook into indicated st, yo, pull up a loop to the same height (3 loops on hook), yo and insert hook into same st, yo, pull up a loop to the same height (5 loops on hook), pinch first loop to secure then yo and pull through all 5 loops on the hook, insert hook into pinched st, yo and pull through (2 loops on hook), yo and pull through rem 2 loops on the hook

J-st = Jasmine Stitch: pull up a loop (around ¾in or 2cm tall), [yo and insert hook, yo, pull up a loop to the same height] twice into top of last st worked (first puff st made, 5 loops on the hook), [yo and insert hook into next sp between puff sts, yo, pull up a loop to the same height] twice (second puff st made, 9 loops on the hook), [yo and insert hook into next sp between puff sts, yo, pull up a loop to the same height] twice (third puff st made, 13 loops on the hook), pinch first loop on hook to secure, yo and pull through all 13 loops on the hook, insert hook into pinched loop, yo and pull through (2 loops on the hook), yo and pull through rem 2 loops on the hook

Pattern note
Jasmine stitch is made up of connected puff stitches. For this stitch we don't start with a traditional foundation chain; we are going to work a series of puff stitches to build the correct shape.

Colour
Blush Pink

SQUARES & SHAPES

In this section you will find a selection of my favourite squares and shapes. You can make several of these in order to create your own customized projects, and you'll also find some half and quarter variations that can be used to 'square off' projects if needed.

Throughout this section, both US and UK terms are given - US is first, with the UK term following in italics and within round brackets.

WHAT YOU'LL FIND FOR EACH SHAPE

Skill level: This will state whether it's classed as beginner, intermediate or advanced. Please note that this is just a guide. I'd always encourage you to give it a go!

Stitches used: A list of stitches that are used within the overall stitch pattern. Refer to the 'Abbreviations' section on pages 171–175 if you need to. There may be some additional information about any special stitches used.

Pattern notes: These give you important information to help you create the shape.

Crochet chart: A diagram made up of a series of symbols that shows both how to work the shape and what the finished shape looks like. Each chart includes a symbol key, so you can see what each symbol represents.

Instructions: These detail how to create the shape in crochet shorthand. Depending on the shape, advice is given on any repeats too. Where increases and decreases occur, stitch counts are provided – these are highlighted in grey, and inside rounded brackets. 'Turn' refers to flipping the shape so that the side once facing away from you is now in front.

Single-colour Granny Square

Skill level
Beginner

Stitches used
ch, sl st, dc (*UK tr*)

Pattern notes
- In my last book, I gave you a super simple granny square pattern which is brilliant for absolute beginners. This one is a little different and has a few adjustments to take your granny squares to the next level.
- You can fasten your yarn off at the end of any round after Round 2 to make your square as big or small as you like.

Colour
Stormy Grey

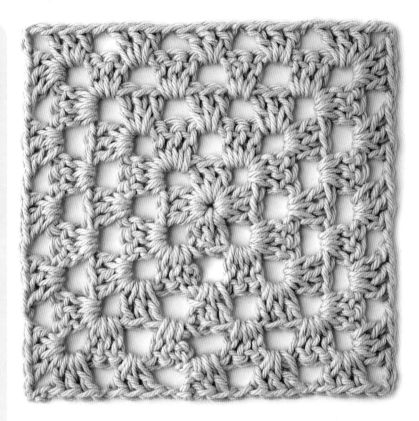

INSTRUCTIONS

4 ch, sl st into fourth ch from hook to form a ring.

Round 1: 3 ch (counts as dc (*UK tr*) here and throughout), into ring work 2 dc (*UK 2 tr*), 3 ch, *3 dc (*UK 3 tr*), 3 ch, rep from * twice more, join with sl st into top of 3-ch. Turn.
(12 dc (*UK 12 tr*), 4 3-ch sps.)

Round 2: sl st into next ch sp, 3 ch, [2 dc (*UK 2 tr*), 3 ch, 3 dc (*UK 3 tr*)] in same 3-ch sp, 1 ch, *[3 dc (*UK 3 tr*), 3 ch, 3 dc (*UK 3 tr*)] in next 3-ch sp, 1 ch, rep from * twice more, join with sl st into top of 3-ch. Turn.
(24 dc (*UK 24 tr*), 4 3-ch sps, 4 1-ch sps.)

Round 3: sl st into next ch sp, 3 ch, 2 dc (*UK 2 tr*) in same ch-sp, 1 ch, *[3 dc (*UK 3 tr*), 3 ch, 3 dc (*UK 3 tr*)] in 3-ch sp, 1 ch, skip 3 sts, 3 dc (*UK 3 tr*) in ch sp, 1 ch, skip 3 sts, rep from * twice more, [3 dc (*UK 3 tr*), 3 ch, 3 dc (*UK 3 tr*)] in 3-ch sp, 1 ch, skip 3 sts, join with sl st into top of 3-ch. Turn.
(36 dc (*UK 36 tr*), 4 3-ch sps, 8 1-ch sps.)

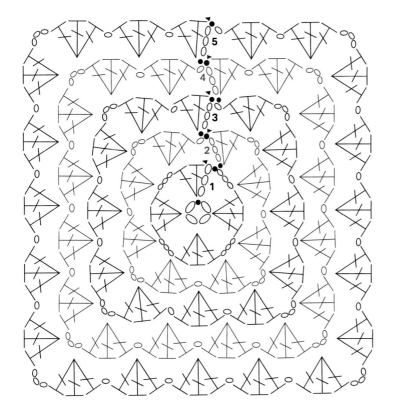

Symbol key

◄   direction to work

○   chain (ch)

●   slip stitch (sl st)

T   double crochet/
     UK treble crochet
     (dc/*UK tr*)

Round 4: sl st into next ch sp, 3 ch, 2 dc (*UK 2 tr*) in same sp, 1 ch, skip 3 sts, *[3 dc (*UK 3 tr*), 3 ch, 3 dc (*UK 3 tr*)] in 3-ch sp, 1 ch, [skip 3 sts, 3 dc (*UK 3 tr*) in ch sp, 1 ch) twice, skip 3 sts, rep from * twice more, [3 dc (*UK 3 tr*)] in 3-ch sp, 1 ch, skip 3 sts, 3 dc (*UK 3 tr*) in ch sp, 1 ch, skip 3 sts, join with sl st into top of 3-ch. Turn.

(48 dc (*UK 48 tr*), 4 3-ch sps, 12 1-ch sps.)

Round 5: sl st into next ch sp, 3 ch, 2 dc (*UK 2 tr*) in same ch sp, 1 ch, [skip 3 sts, 3 dc (*UK 3 tr*) in ch-sp, 1 ch] to corner 3-ch sp, skip 3 sts, *[3 dc (*UK 3 tr*), 3 ch, 3 dc (*UK 3 tr*)] in 3-ch sp, 1 ch, skip 3 sts, [3 dc (*UK 3 tr*) in ch sp, 1 ch, skip 3 sts] to corner 3-ch sp, rep from * twice more, [3 dc (*UK 3 tr*), 3 ch, 3 dc (*UK 3 tr*)] in 3-ch sp, [1 ch, skip 3 sts, 3 dc (*UK 3 tr*) in ch sp] to end, 1 ch, join with sl st into top of 3-ch. Turn.

(60 dc (*UK 60 tr*), 4 3-ch sps, 16 1-ch sps.)

Rep Round 5 until desired size.

Fasten off and sew in ends.

Multi-coloured Granny Square

Skill level
Beginner

Stitches used
ch, sl st, dc (*UK tr*)

Pattern notes
- You can fasten your yarn off at the end of any round after Round 2 to make your square as big or small as you like.
- You can change colours as you please with your granny squares. Use one, two, three or more colours to get your desired look.

Colours
Stormy Grey (A), Blush Pink (B), Sea Foam (C), Vanilla Cream (D)

INSTRUCTIONS

With yarn A, 4 ch, sl st into fourth ch from hook to form a ring.

Round 1: 3 ch (counts as dc (*UK tr*) here and throughout), into ring work 2 dc (*UK tr*), 3 ch, *3 dc (*UK 3 tr*), 3 ch, rep from * twice more, join with sl st into top of 3-ch. Fasten off.

(12 dc (*UK 12 tr*), 4 3-ch sps.)

Turn. Join yarn B in any 3-ch sp.

Round 2: 3 ch, [2 dc (*UK 2 tr*), 3 ch, 3 dc (*UK 3 tr*)] in same 3-ch sp, 1 ch, *[3 dc (*UK 3 tr*), 3 ch, 3 dc (*UK 3 tr*)] in next 3-ch sp, 1 ch, rep from * twice more, join with sl st into top of 3-ch. Fasten off.

(24 dc (*UK 24 tr*), 4 3-ch sps, 4 1-ch sps.)

Turn. Join yarn C in any 3-ch sp.

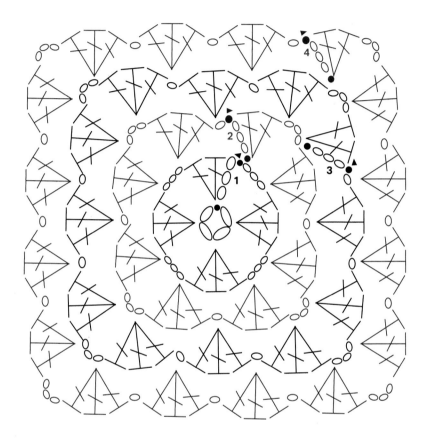

Symbol key

◄   direction to work

○   chain (ch)

●   slip stitch (sl st)

⊤   double crochet/
      UK treble crochet
      (dc/*UK tr*)

Round 3: 3 ch, [2 dc (*UK 2 tr*), 3 ch, 3 dc (*UK 3 tr*)] in same 3-ch sp, 1 ch,
*skip 3 sts, 3 dc (*UK 3 tr*) in ch sp, 1 ch, skip 3 sts, [3 dc (*UK 3 tr*), 3 ch,
3 dc (*UK 3 tr*)] in next 3-ch sp, 1 ch, rep from * twice more, skip 3 sts,
3 dc (*UK 3 tr*) in ch sp, 1 ch, skip 3 sts, join with sl st into top of 3-ch. Fasten off.
(36 dc (*UK 36 tr*), 4 3-ch sps, 8 1-ch sps.)
Turn. Join yarn D in any 3-ch sp.

Round 4: 3 ch, [2 dc (*UK 2 tr*), 3 ch, 3 dc (*UK 3 tr*)] in same 3-ch sp, 1 ch,
skip 3 sts, *[3 dc (*UK 3 tr*) in ch sp, 1 ch, skip 3 sts] to corner 3-ch sp,
[3 dc (*UK 3 tr*), 3 ch, 3 dc (*UK 3 tr*)] in 3-ch sp, 1 ch, skip 3 sts, rep from *
twice more, [3 dc (*UK 3 tr*) in ch sp, 1 ch, skip 3 sts] to end, join with sl st
into top of 3-ch. Fasten off.
(48 dc (*UK 48 tr*), 4 3-ch sps, 12 1-ch sps.)
Turn. Rep Round 4 until desired size, turning work after each round and
changing colours as needed.
Fasten off and sew in ends.

Solid Granny Square

Skill level
Beginner

Stitches used
ch, sl st, dc (*UK tr*)

Colour
Sea Foam

INSTRUCTIONS

4 ch, sl st into fourth ch from hook to form a ring.

Round 1: 3 ch (counts as dc (*UK tr*) here and throughout), into ring work 2 dc (*UK 2 tr*), 3 ch, *3 dc (*UK 3 tr*), 3 ch, rep from * twice more, join with sl st into top of 3-ch. Turn.
(12 dc (*UK 12 tr*), 4 ch sps.)

Round 2: 3 ch, [2 dc (*UK 2 tr*), 3 ch, 2 dc (*UK 2 tr*)] in 3-ch sp, *dc (*UK tr*) in next 3 sts, [2 dc (*UK 2 tr*), 3 ch, 2 dc (*UK 2 tr*)] in 3-ch sp, rep from * twice more, dc (*UK tr*) in last 2 sts, join with sl st into top of 3-ch. Turn.
(28 dc (*UK 28 tr*), 4 ch sps.)

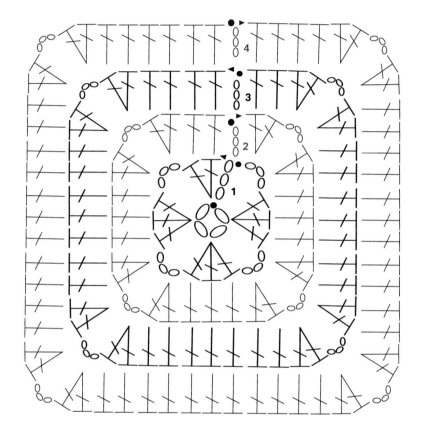

Symbol key

◄   direction to work

○   chain (ch)

●   slip stitch (sl st)

†   double crochet/
UK treble crochet
(dc/*UK tr*)

Round 3: 3 ch, dc (*UK tr*) in next 4 sts, *[2 dc (*UK 2 tr*), 3 ch, 2 dc (*UK 2 tr*)] in 3-ch sp, dc (*UK tr*) in next 7 sts, rep from * twice more, [2 dc (*UK 2 tr*), 3 ch, 2 dc (*UK 2 tr*)] in 3-ch sp, dc (*UK tr*) in last 2 sts, join with sl st into top of 3-ch. Turn.
(44 dc (*UK 44 tr*), 4 ch sps.)

Round 4: 3 ch, dc (*UK tr*) in each st to 3-ch sp, *[2 dc (*UK 2 tr*), 3 ch, 2 dc (*UK 2 tr*)] in 3-ch sp, dc (*UK tr*) in each st to 3-ch sp, rep from * twice more, [2 dc (*UK 2 tr*), 3 ch, 2 dc (*UK 2 tr*)] in 3-ch sp, dc (*UK tr*) in each st to end, join with sl st into top of 3-ch. Turn.
(60 dc (*UK 60 tr*), 4 ch sps.)

Rep Round 4 until desired size.

Fasten off and sew in ends.

Granny Triangle
(HALF GRANNY SQUARE)

Skill level
Beginner

Stitches used
ch, sl st, dc (*UK tr*)

Colour
Pistachio Green

Symbol key

◄   direction to work

○   chain (ch)

●   slip stitch (sl st)

†   double crochet/
      UK treble crochet
      (**dc**/*UK tr*)

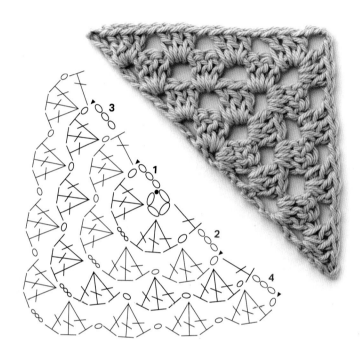

INSTRUCTIONS

4 ch, sl st into fourth ch from hook to form a ring.

Row 1: 4 ch (counts as dc (*UK tr*) and 1 ch here and throughout), into ring work 3 dc (*UK 3 tr*), 3 ch, 3 dc (*UK 3 tr*), 1 ch, dc (*UK tr*). Turn.

(8 dc (*UK 8 tr*), 1 3-ch sp, 2 1-ch sps.)

Row 2: 4 ch, 3 dc (*UK 3 tr*) in 1-ch sp, 1 ch, [3 dc (*UK 3 tr*), 1 ch, 3 dc (*UK 3 tr*)] in 3-ch sp, 1 ch, [3 dc (*UK 3 tr*), 3 ch, dc (*UK tr*)] in last 1-ch sp. Turn.

(14 dc (*UK 14 tr*), 1 3-ch sp, 4 1-ch sps.)

Row 3: 4 ch, 3 dc (*UK 3 tr*) in 1-ch sp, 1 ch, 3 dc (*UK 3 tr*) in next 1-ch sp, 1 ch, [3 dc (*UK 3 tr*), 3 ch, 3 dc (*UK 3 tr*)] in 3-ch sp, 1 ch, 3 dc (*UK 3 tr*) in next 1-ch sp, 1 ch, [3 dc (*UK 3 tr*), 1 ch, dc (*UK tr*)] in last 1-ch sp. Turn.

(20 dc (*UK 20 tr*), 1 3-ch sp, 6 1-ch sps.)

Row 4: 4 ch, 3 dc (*UK 3 tr*) in 1-ch sp, [1 ch, 3 dc (*UK 3 tr*) in next 1-ch sp] to 3-ch sp, 1 ch, [3 dc (*UK 3 tr*), 3 ch, 3 dc (*UK 3 tr*)] in 3-ch sp, [1 ch, 3 dc (*UK 3 tr*) in next 1-ch sp] to last 1-ch sp, 1 ch, [3 dc (*UK 3 tr*), 1 ch, dc (*UK tr*)] in last 1-ch sp. Turn.

(26 dc (*UK 26 tr*), 1 3-ch sp, 8 1-ch sps.)

Rep Row 4 until desired size.

Fasten off and sew in ends.

Solid Granny Triangle
(SOLID HALF GRANNY SQUARE)

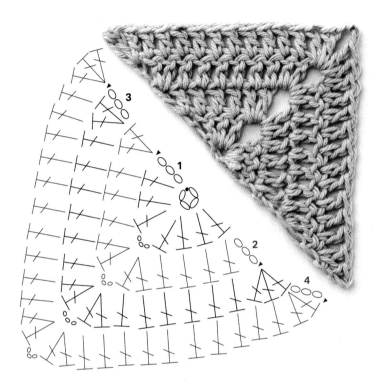

Skill level
Beginner

Stitches used
ch, sl st, dc (*UK tr*)

Colour
Pistachio Green

Symbol key

◄   direction to work

○   chain (ch)

●   slip stitch (sl st)

⊤   double crochet/
UK treble crochet
(**dc**/*UK tr*)

INSTRUCTIONS

4 ch, sl st into fourth ch from hook to form a ring.

Row 1: 3 ch (counts as dc (*UK tr*) here and throughout) into ring work 3 dc (*UK 3 tr*), 3 ch, 4 dc (*UK 4 tr*). Turn.

(8 dc (*UK 8 tr*), 1 3-ch sp.)

Row 2: 3 ch, dc (*UK tr*) in st at base of 3-ch, dc (*UK tr*) in next 3 sts, [2 dc (*UK 2 tr*), 3 ch, 2 dc (*UK 2 tr*)] in 3-ch sp, dc (*UK tr*) in next 3 sts, 2 dc (*UK 2 tr*) in top of 3-ch. Turn.

(14 dc (*UK 14 tr*), 1 3-ch sp.)

Row 3: 3 ch, 2 dc (*UK 2 tr*) in st at base of 3-ch, dc (*UK tr*) in each st to 3-ch sp, [2 dc (*UK 2 tr*), 3 ch, 2 dc (*UK 2 tr*)] in 3-ch sp, dc (*UK tr*) in each st to last st, 3 dc (*UK 3 tr*) in top of 3-ch. Turn.

(22 dc (*UK 22 tr*), 1 3-ch sp.)

Row 4: rep Row 3.

(30 dc (*UK 30 tr*), 1 3-ch sp).

Rep Row 3 until desired size.

Fasten off and sew in ends.

Super Solid Granny Square

Skill level
Beginner

Stitches used
ch, sl st, dc (*UK tr*), tr (*UK dtr*)

Colour
Blush Pink

INSTRUCTIONS

Either make a magic ring/adjustable loop (for a closed centre) or 4 ch then sl st into fourth ch from hook to form a ring (for an open centre).

Round 1: 3 ch (counts as dc (*UK tr*) here and throughout), into ring work 2 dc (*UK 2 tr*), tr (*UK dtr*), [3 dc (*UK 3 tr*), tr (*UK dtr*)] three times, join with sl st into top of 3-ch.
(16 sts.)

Round 2: 3 ch, dc (*UK tr*) in next 2 sts, *[dc (*UK tr*), tr (*UK dtr*), dc (*UK tr*)] in next tr (*UK dtr*), dc (*UK tr*) in next 3 sts, rep from * twice more, [dc (*UK tr*), tr (*UK dtr*), dc (*UK tr*)] in last tr (*UK dtr*), join with sl st into top of 3-ch.
(24 sts.)

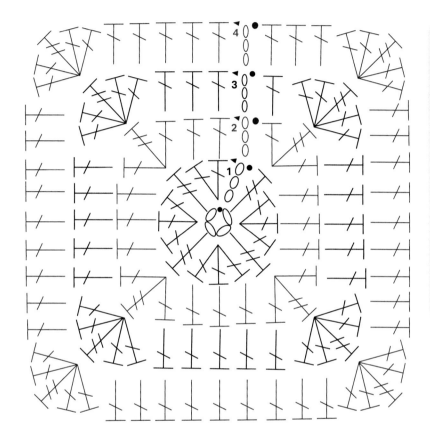

Symbol key

◀ direction to work

○ chain (ch)

● slip stitch (sl st)

⊤ double crochet/
UK treble crochet
(**dc**/*UK tr*)

⊤ treble crochet/
UK double treble crochet
(**tr**/*UK dtr*)

Round 3: 3 ch, dc (*UK tr*) in next 3 sts, *[2 dc (*UK 2 tr*), tr (*UK dtr*),
2 dc (*UK 2 tr*)] in next tr (*UK dtr*), dc (*UK tr*) in next 5 sts, rep from *
twice more, [2 dc (*UK 2 tr*), tr (*UK dtr*), 2 dc (*UK 2 tr*)] in next st,
dc (*UK tr*) in last st, join with sl st into top of 3-ch.
(40 sts.)

Round 4: 3 ch, *dc (*UK tr*) in each st to corner tr (*UK dtr*), [2 dc (*UK tr*),
tr (*UK dtr*), 2 dc (*UK 2 tr*)] in corner tr (*UK dtr*), rep from * three more times,
dc (*UK tr*) in each st to end, join with sl st into top of 3 ch.
(56 sts.)

Rep Round 4 until desired size.

Fasten off and sew in ends.

Filet Square

Skill level
Beginner

Stitches used
ch, sl st, dc (*UK tr*)

Colour
Blush Pink

INSTRUCTIONS

4 ch, sl st into fourth ch from hook to form a ring.

Round 1: 3 ch (counts as dc (*UK tr*) here and throughout), into ring work 2 dc (*UK 2 tr*), 3 ch, *3 dc (*UK 3 tr*), 3 ch, rep from * twice more, join with sl st into top of 3-ch. Turn. (12 dc (*UK 12 tr*), 4 3-ch sps.)

Round 2: 3 ch, [2 dc (*UK 2 tr*), 3 ch, 2 dc (UK 2 tr)] in 3-ch sp, *dc (*UK tr*) in next 3 sts, [2 dc (*UK 2 tr*), 3 ch, 2 dc (*UK 2 tr*)] in 3-ch sp, rep from * twice more, dc (*UK tr*) in last 2 sts, join with sl st into top of 3-ch. Turn. (28 dc (*UK 28 tr*), 4 3-ch sps.)

Round 3: 4 ch (counts as dc (*UK tr*) and 1 ch here and throughout), skip 1 st, dc (*UK tr*) in next 3 sts, *[2 dc (*UK 2 tr*), 3 ch, 2 dc (*UK 2 tr*)] in 3-ch sp, dc (*UK tr*) in next 3 sts, 1 ch, skip 1 st, dc (*UK tr*) in next 3 sts, rep from * twice more, [2 dc (*UK 2 tr*), 3 ch, 2 dc (*UK 2 tr*)] in 3-ch sp, dc in last 2 sts, join with sl st into third of 4-ch. Turn. (40 dc (*UK 40 tr*), 4 3-ch sps, 4 1-ch sps.)

Round 4: 4 ch, skip a st, dc (*UK tr*) in next 3 sts, *[2 dc (*UK 2 tr*), 3 ch, 2 dc (*UK 2 tr*)] in 3-ch sp, dc (*UK tr*) in next 3 sts, 1 ch, skip 1 st, dc (*UK tr*) in next st, dc (*UK tr*) in ch-1 sp, dc (*UK tr*) in next st, 1 ch, skip 1 st, dc (*UK tr*) in next 3 sts, repeat from * twice more, [2 dc (*UK 2 tr*), 3 ch, 2 dc (*UK 2 tr*)] in 3-ch sp, dc (*UK tr*) in next 3 sts, 1 ch, skip 1 st, dc (*UK tr*) into next st, dc (*UK tr*) in 1-ch sp, join with sl st into third of 4-ch. Turn. (52 dc (*UK 52 tr*), 4 3-ch sps, 8 1-ch sps.)

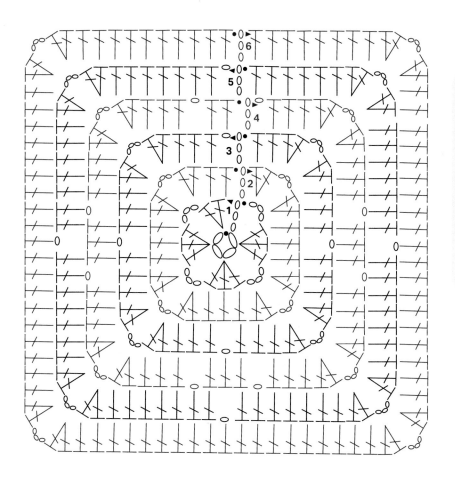

Symbol key

◄   direction to work

◯   chain (ch)

●   slip stitch (sl st)

┬   double crochet/
    UK treble crochet
    (dc/*UK tr*)

Round 5: 4 ch, skip a st, dc (*UK tr*) in next st, dc (*UK tr*) in 1-ch sp, dc (*UK tr*) in next 5 sts, *[2 dc (*UK 2 tr*), 3 ch, 2 dc (*UK 2 tr*)] in 3-ch sp, dc (*UK tr*) in next 5 sts, dc (*UK tr*) in 1-ch sp, dc (*UK tr*) in next st, 1 ch, skip 1 st, dc (*UK tr*) in next st, dc (*UK tr*) in 1-ch sp, dc (*UK tr*) in next 5 sts, rep from * twice more, [2 dc (*UK 2 tr*), 3 ch, 2 dc (*UK 2 tr*)] in 3-ch sp, dc (*UK tr*) in next 5 sts, dc (*UK tr*) in 1-ch sp, join with sl st into third of 4-ch. Turn.
(72 dc (*UK 72 tr*), 4 3-ch sps, 4 1-ch sps.)

Round 6: 3 ch, dc (*UK tr*) in next 8 sts, *[2 dc (*UK 2 tr*), 3 ch, 2 dc (*UK 2 tr*)] in 3-ch sp, dc (*UK tr*) in next 9 sts, dc (*UK tr*) in 1-ch sp, dc (*UK tr*) in next 9 sts, repeat from * twice more, [2 dc (*UK 2 tr*), 3 ch, 2 dc (*UK 2 tr*)] in 3-ch sp, dc (*UK tr*) in next 9 sts, dc (*UK tr*) in 1-ch sp, join with sl st into top of 3-ch. Turn.
(92 dc (*UK 92 tr*), 4 3-ch sps.)
Fasten off and sew in ends.

Granny Rectangle

Skill level
Beginner

Multiples
3 + 2

Stitches used
ch, sl st, dc (*UK tr*)

Pattern note
If you wish to increase the size of the centre of your rectangle, you can increase your chain using the multiples provided above.

Colour
Stormy Grey

INSTRUCTIONS

17 ch.

Round 1: 2 dc (*UK 2 tr*) in third ch from hook (skipped 2-ch counts as dc (*UK tr*)), 3 ch, 3 dc (*UK 3 tr*) in next ch, *1 ch, skip 2 ch, 3 dc (*UK 3 tr*) in next ch, rep from * until 1 ch rem, 3 ch, 3 dc (*UK 3 tr*) in last ch, 3 ch, turn work so you are working on the underside of the foundation ch, skip first ch, [3 dc (*UK 3 tr*) in next ch, 1 ch, skip 2 ch] to end, working final rep as 3 dc (*UK 3 tr*) in next ch, 3 ch, join with sl st into top of 3-ch. Turn.

(12 clusters, 4 3-ch sps, 8 1-ch sps.)

Round 2: 3 ch (counts as dc (*UK tr*) here and throughout), [2 dc (*UK 2 tr*), 3 ch, 3 dc (*UK 3 tr*)] in 3-ch sp, 1 ch, *3 dc (*UK 3 tr*) in next ch sp, 1 ch, rep from * to 3-ch sp, [3 dc (*UK 3 tr*), 3 ch, 3 dc (*UK 3 tr*) in next 3-ch sp, 1 ch] twice, [3 dc (*UK 3 tr*) in next ch-sp, 1 ch] to 3-ch sp, [3 dc (*UK 3 tr*), 3 ch, 3 dc (*UK 3 tr*)] in 3-ch sp, 1 ch, join with sl st into top of 3-ch. Turn.

(16 clusters, 4 3-ch sps, 12 1-ch sps.)

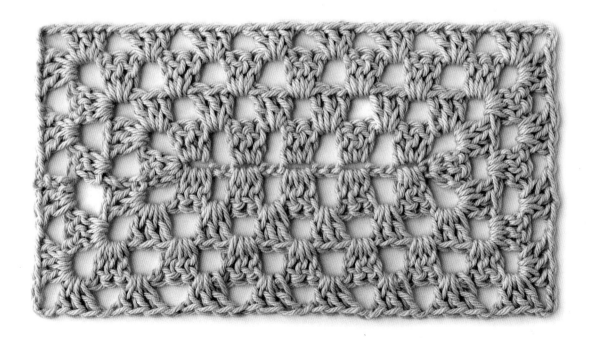

Round 3: 3 ch, 2 dc (*UK 2 tr*) in 1-ch sp, 1 ch, [3 dc (*UK 3 tr*), 3 ch, 3 dc (*UK 3 tr*)] in 3-ch sp, *1 ch [3 dc (*UK 3 tr*) in next ch-sp, 1 ch] to 3-ch sp, [3 dc (*UK 3 tr*), 3 ch, 3 dc (*UK 3 tr*)] in 3-ch sp, rep from * to end, join with sl st in top of 3-ch. Turn.

(20 clusters, 4 3-ch sps, 16 1-ch sps.)

Round 4: 3 ch, 2 dc (*UK 2 tr*) in 1-ch sp, [1 ch, 3 dc (*UK 3 tr*)] to corner 3-ch sp, 3 ch, 3 dc (*UK 3 tr*)] in same ch sp as previous st, *[3 dc (*UK 3 tr*) in next 1-ch sp, 1 ch] to 3-ch sp, [3 dc (*UK 3 tr*), 3 ch, 3 dc (*UK 3 tr*)] in 3-ch sp, 1 ch, rep from * three more times, [3 dc (*UK 3 tr*) in next 1-ch sp, 1 ch] to end, join with sl st in top of 3-ch. Turn.

(24 clusters, 4 3-ch sps, 20 1-ch sps.)

Rep Round 4 until desired size.

Fasten off and sew in ends.

Symbol key

◄   direction to work

○   chain (ch)

●   slip stitch (sl st)

⊤   double crochet/
     UK treble crochet
     (dc/*UK tr*)

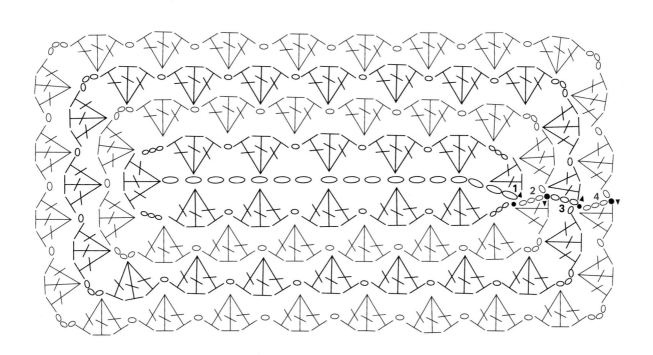

Granny Hexagon

Skill level
Intermediate

Stitches used
ch, sl st, dc (*UK tr*)

Pattern note
'Granny set' refers to 3 dc (*UK 3 tr*)
worked into one sp.

Colour
Sea Foam

INSTRUCTIONS

4 ch, sl st into fourth ch from hook to form a ring.

Round 1: 3 ch (counts as dc (*UK tr*) here and throughout), into ring work 2 dc (*UK 2 tr*), [1 ch, 3 dc (*UK 3 tr*)] five times, 1 ch, join with sl st into top of 3-ch. Turn.
(6 granny sets, 6 ch sps.)

Round 2: 3 ch, [2 dc (*UK 2 tr*), 1 ch, 3 dc (*UK 3 tr*)] in same ch sp, *[3 dc (*UK 3 tr*), 1 ch, 3 dc (*UK 3 tr*)] in next ch sp, rep from * four more times, join with sl st into top of 3-ch. Turn.
(12 granny sets, 6 ch sps.)

Round 3: 3 ch, 2 dc (*UK 2 tr*) in sp between granny sets at base of 3-ch, *[3 dc (*UK 3 tr*), 1 ch, 3 dc (*UK 3 tr*)] in next ch sp, 3 dc (*UK 3 tr*) in next sp between granny sets, rep from * four more times, [3 dc (*UK 3 tr*), 1 ch, 3 dc (*UK 3 tr*)] in next ch sp, join with sl st into top of 3-ch. Turn.
(18 granny sets, 6 ch sps.)

Round 4: 3 ch, 2 dc (*UK 2 tr*) in sp between granny sets at base of 3-ch, *[3 dc (*UK 3 tr*), 1 ch, 3 dc (*UK 3 tr*)] in next ch sp, [3 dc (*UK 3 tr*) in next sp between granny sets] to next ch sp, rep from * four more times, [3 dc (*UK 3 tr*), 1 ch, 3 dc (*UK 3 tr*)] in next ch sp, 3 dc (*UK 3 tr*) in next sp between granny sets, join with sl st into top of 3-ch. Turn.
(24 granny sets, 6 ch sps.)

Symbol key

◄   direction to work

○   chain (ch)

●   slip stitch (sl st)

T   double crochet/
     UK treble crochet
     (**dc**/*UK tr*)

Round 5: 3 ch, 2 dc (*UK 2 tr*) in sp between granny sets
at base of 3-ch, [3 dc (*UK 3 tr*) in next sp between granny
sets] to next ch sp, *[3 dc (*UK 3 tr*), 1 ch, 3 dc (*UK 3 tr*)] in
next ch sp, [3 dc (*UK 3 tr*) in next sp between granny sets]
to next ch sp, rep from * four more times, [3 dc (*UK 3 tr*),
1 ch, 3 dc (*UK 3 tr*)] in next ch sp, [3 dc (*UK 3 tr*) in next sp
between granny sets] to end, join with sl st into top of
3-ch. Turn.
(30 granny sets, 6 ch sps.)
Rep Round 5 until desired size.
Fasten off and sew in ends.

Granny Half Hexagon
– HORIZONTAL

Skill level
Intermediate

Stitches used
ch, sl st, dc (*UK tr*)

Pattern note
'Granny set' refers to 3 dc (*UK 3 tr*) worked into one sp.

Colour
Blush Pink

Symbol key

◄   direction to work

○   chain (ch)

●   slip stitch (sl st)

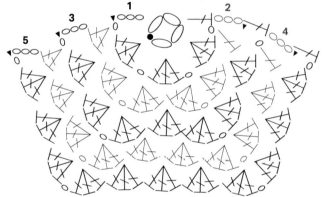   double crochet/*UK treble crochet* (dc/*UK tr*)

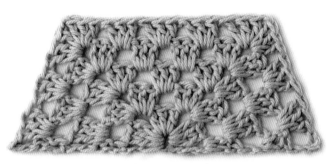

INSTRUCTIONS

4 ch, sl st into fourth ch from hook to form a ring.

Row 1: 4 ch (counts as dc (*UK tr*) and 1 ch here and throughout), into ring work [3 dc (*UK 3 tr*), 1 ch] three times, dc (*UK tr*). Turn.

(3 granny sets, 2 dc (*UK 2 tr*), 4 ch sps.)

Row 2: 3 ch (counts as dc (*UK tr*) here and throughout), dc (*UK tr*) in ch sp, *[3 dc (*UK 3 tr*), 1 ch, 3 dc (*UK 3 tr*)] in next ch sp, rep from * once more, 2 dc (*UK 2 tr*) in next ch sp. Turn.

(4 granny sets, 4 dc (*UK 3 tr*), 2 ch sps.)

Row 3: 4 ch, 3 dc (*UK 3 tr*) in next sp between granny sets, *[3 dc (*UK 3 tr*), 1 ch, 3 dc (*UK 3 tr*)] in next ch sp, 3 dc (*UK 3 tr*) in next sp between granny sets, rep from * once more, 1 ch, skip next st, dc (*UK tr*) in top of 3-ch. Turn.

(7 granny sets, 2 dc (*UK 2 tr*), 4 ch sps.)

Row 4: 3 ch, dc (*UK tr*) in ch sp. *[3 dc (*UK 3 tr*) in next space between granny sets] to ch sp, [3 dc (*UK 3 tr*), 1 ch, 3 dc (*UK 3 tr*)] in next ch sp, rep from * once more, [3 dc (*UK 3 tr*) in next sp between granny sets] to ch sp, 2 dc (*UK 2 tr*) in ch sp. Turn.

(8 granny sets, 4 dc (*UK 4 tr*), 2 ch sps.)

Row 5: 4 ch, *[3 dc (*UK 3 tr*) in next sp between granny sets] to ch sp, [3 dc (*UK 3 tr*), 1 ch, 3 dc (*UK 3 tr*)] in next ch sp, rep from * once more, [3 dc (*UK 3 tr*) in next sp between granny sets] to last 2 dc (*UK 2 tr*), 1 ch, skip next st, dc (*UK tr*) in top of 3-ch. Turn.

(11 granny sets, 4 dc (*UK 4 tr*), 2 ch-sps.)

Rep Rounds 4 and 5 until desired size.

Fasten off and sew in ends.

Granny Half Hexagon
– VERTICAL

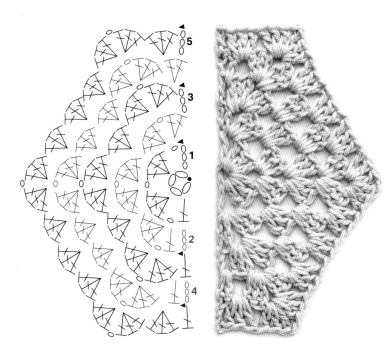

Skill level
Intermediate

Stitches used
ch, sl st, dc (*UK tr*)

Pattern note
'Granny set' refers to 3 dc (*UK 3 tr*) worked into one sp.

Colour
Vanilla Cream

Symbol key

◄   direction to work

○   chain (ch)

●   slip stitch (sl st)

⊤   double crochet/
     UK treble crochet
     (**dc**/*UK tr*)

INSTRUCTIONS

4 ch, sl st into fourth ch from hook to form a ring.

Row 1: 4 ch (counts as dc (*UK tr*) and 1 ch), into the ring work [3 dc (*UK 3 tr*), 1 ch] twice, dc (*UK tr*). Turn.
(2 granny sets, 2 dc (*UK 2 tr*), 3 ch sps.)

Row 2: 3 ch (counts as dc (*UK tr*) here and throughout), [dc (*UK tr*), 1 ch, 3 dc (*UK 3 tr*)] in ch sp, [3 dc (*UK 3 tr*), 1 ch, 3 dc (*UK 3 tr*)] in next ch sp, [3 dc (*UK 3 tr*), 1 ch, 2 dc (*UK 2 tr*)] in next ch sp. Turn.
(4 granny sets, 4 dc (*UK 4 tr*), 3 ch sps.)

Row 3: 3 ch, *[3 dc (*UK 3 tr*), 1 ch, 3 dc (*UK 3 tr*)] in next ch sp, 3 dc (*UK 3 tr*) in next sp between granny sets, rep from * once more, [3 dc (*UK 3 tr*), 1 ch, 3 dc (*UK 3 tr*)] in next ch sp, skip next st, dc (*UK tr*) in top of 3-ch. Turn.
(8 granny sets, 2 dc (*UK 2 tr*), 3 ch sps.)

Row 4: 3 ch, dc (*UK tr*) in sp between sts at base of 3-ch, *[3 dc (*UK 3 tr*), 1 ch, 3 dc (*UK 3 tr*)] in next ch sp, [3 dc (*UK 3 tr*) in next sp between granny sets] twice, rep from * once more, [3 dc (*UK 3 tr*), 1 ch, 3 dc (*UK 3 tr*)] in next sp between granny sets, skip 3 sts, 2 dc (*UK 2 tr*) in top of 3-ch. Turn.
(10 granny sets, 4 dc (*UK 4 tr*), 3 ch sps.)

Row 5: 3 ch, *[3 dc (*UK 3 tr*) in next sp between granny sets] to next ch sp, [3 dc (*UK 3 tr*), 1 ch, 3 dc (*UK 3 tr*)] in next ch sp, rep from * twice more, [3 dc (*UK 3 tr*) in next sp between granny sets] to last dc (*UK tr*), dc (*UK tr*) in top of 3-ch. Turn.
(14 granny sets, 2 dc (*UK 4 tr*), 3 ch sps.)

Rep Rounds 4 and 5 until desired size.

Fasten off and sew in ends.

Solid Hexagon

Skill level
Beginner

Stitches used
ch, sl st, dc (*UK tr*)

Colour
Vanilla Cream

INSTRUCTIONS

4 ch, sl st into fourth ch from hook to form a ring.

Round 1: 3 ch (counts as a dc (*UK tr*) here and throughout), into ring work dc (*UK tr*), [1 ch, 2 dc (*UK 2 tr*)] five times, 1 ch, sl st into top of 3-ch. Turn. (12 dc (*UK 12 tr*), 6 1-ch sps.)

Round 2: 3 ch, *[dc (*UK tr*), 1 ch, dc (*UK tr*)] in ch-sp, dc (*UK tr*) in next 2 sts, rep from * four more times, [dc (*UK tr*), 1 ch, dc (*UK tr*)] in ch sp, dc (*UK tr*) in last st, sl st into top of 3-ch. Turn. (24 dc (*UK 24 tr*), 6 1-ch sps.)

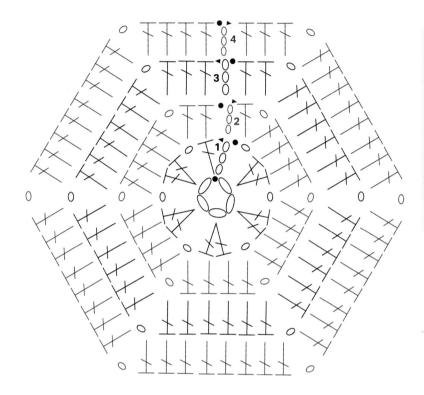

Symbol key

◀   direction to work

○   chain (ch)

●   slip stitch (sl st)

┬   double crochet/
     UK treble crochet
     (dc/*UK tr***)**

Round 3: 3 ch, dc (*UK tr*) in next 2 sts, *[dc (*UK tr*), 1 ch, dc (*UK tr*)] in ch sp, dc (*UK tr*) in next 4 sts, rep from * four more times, [dc (*UK tr*), 1 ch, dc (*UK tr*)] in ch-sp, dc (*UK tr*) in last st, sl st into top of 3-ch. Turn. (36 dc (*UK 36 tr*), 6 1-ch sps.)

Round 4: 3 ch, dc (*UK tr*) in each st to ch sp, *[dc (*UK tr*), 1 ch, dc (*UK tr*)] in ch sp, dc (*UK tr*) in each st to ch sp, rep from * four more times, [dc (*UK tr*), 1 ch, dc (*UK tr*)] in ch sp, dc (*UK tr*) in each st to end, sl st into top of 3-ch. Turn. (48 dc (*UK 48 tr*), 6 1-ch sps.)

Rep Round 4 until desired size.

Fasten off and sew in ends.

Solid Half Hexagon
– HORIZONTAL

Skill level
Intermediate

Stitches used
ch, sl st, dc (*UK tr*)

Colour
Sea Foam

Symbol key

◄   direction to work

○   chain (ch)

●   slip stitch (sl st)

†   double crochet/
     UK treble crochet
     (dc/*UK tr*)

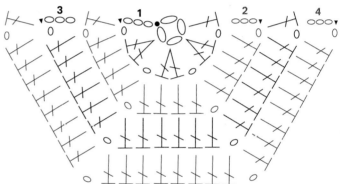

INSTRUCTIONS

4 ch, sl st into fourth ch from hook to form a ring.

Row 1: 4 ch (counts as dc (*UK tr*) and 1 ch), into ring work [2 dc (*UK 2 tr*), 1 ch] three times, dc (*UK tr*). Turn.
(8 dc (*UK 8 tr*), 4 ch sps.)

Row 2: 4 ch, dc (*UK tr*) in ch sp, *dc (*UK tr*) in next 2 sts, [dc (*UK tr*), 1 ch, dc (*UK tr*)] in ch sp, rep from * twice more. Turn.
(14 dc (*UK 14 tr*), 4 ch sps.)

Row 3: 4 ch, dc (*UK tr*) in ch sp, *dc (*UK tr*) in each st to ch sp, [dc (*UK tr*), 1 ch, dc (*UK tr*)] in ch sp, rep from * twice more. Turn.
(20 dc (*UK 20 tr*), 4 ch sps.)

Row 4: rep Row 3.
(26 dc (*UK 26 tr*), 4 ch sps.)

Rep Row 3 until desired size.

Fasten off and sew in ends.

Solid Half Hexagon
– VERTICAL

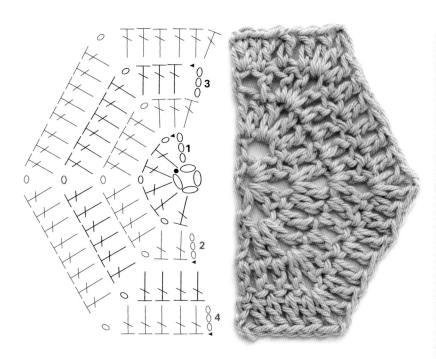

Skill level
Intermediate

Stitches used
ch, sl st, dc (*UK tr*)

Colour
Pistachio Green

Symbol key

◄   direction to work

○   chain (ch)

●   slip stitch (sl st)

T   double crochet/
UK treble crochet
(**dc**/*UK tr*)

INSTRUCTIONS

4 ch, sl st into fourth ch from hook to form a ring.

Row 1: 4 ch (counts as a dc (*UK tr*) and 1 ch), into ring work dc (*UK tr*), *[dc (*UK tr*), 1 ch, dc (*UK tr*)] twice. Turn.
(6 dc (*UK 6 tr*), 3 ch sps.)

Row 2: 3 ch (counts as dc (*UK tr*) here and throughout), dc (*UK tr*) in st at base of 3-ch, *[dc (*UK tr*), 1 ch, dc (*UK tr*)] in ch sp, dc (*UK tr*) in next 2 sts, rep from * once more, [dc (*UK tr*), 1 ch, dc (*UK tr*)] in last 1-ch sp, 2 dc (*UK tr*) in third of 4-ch. Turn.
(14 dc (*UK 14 tr*), 3 ch sps.)

Row 3: 3 ch, dc (*UK tr*) in each st to ch sp, *[dc (*UK tr*), 1 ch, dc (*UK tr*)] in ch sp, dc (*UK tr*) in each st to ch sp, rep from * once more, [dc (*UK tr*), 1 ch, dc (*UK tr*)] in ch sp, dc (*UK tr*) in each st to end. Turn.
(20 dc (*UK 20 tr*), 3 ch sps.)

Row 4: 3 ch, dc (*UK tr*) in st at base of 3-ch, dc (*UK tr*) in each st to ch sp, *[dc (*UK tr*), 1 ch, dc (*UK tr*)] in ch sp, dc (*UK tr*) in each st to ch sp, rep from * once more, [dc (*UK tr*), 1 ch, dc (*UK tr*)] in ch sp, dc (*UK tr*) in each st until 1 st rem, 2 dc (*UK 2 tr*) in top of 3-ch. Turn.
(28 dc (*UK 28 tr*), 3 ch sps.)

Rep Rounds 4 and 5 until desired size.

Fasten off and sew in ends.

Granny Hexagon
– QUARTER

Skill level
Intermediate

Stitches used
ch, sl st, dc (*UK tr*)

Pattern note
'Granny set' refers to 3 dc (*UK 3 tr*) worked into one sp.

Colour
Pistachio

Symbol key

◄   direction to work

○   chain (ch)

●   slip stitch (sl st)

⊤   double crochet/
UK treble crochet
(**dc**/*UK tr*)

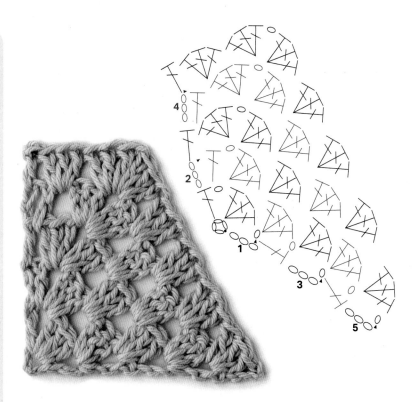

INSTRUCTIONS

4 ch, sl st into fourth ch from hook to form a ring.

Row 1: 4 ch (counts as dc (*UK tr*) and 1 ch here and throughout), into ring work 3 dc (*UK 3 tr*), 1 ch, dc (*UK tr*). Turn.

(1 granny set, 2 dc (*UK 2 tr*), 2 ch sps.)

Row 2: 3 ch (counts as dc (*UK tr*) here and throughout), [dc (*UK tr*), 1 ch, 3 dc (*UK 3 tr*)] in first ch sp, [3 dc (*UK 3 tr*), 1 ch, dc (*UK tr*)] in last ch-sp. Turn.

(2 granny sets, 3 dc (*UK 3 tr*), 2 ch sps.)

Row 3: 4 ch, 3 dc (*UK 3 tr*) in ch sp, 3 dc (*UK 3 tr*) in next sp between granny sets, [3 dc (*UK 3 tr*), 1 ch, 3 dc (*UK 3 tr*)] in last ch sp, skip 1 st, dc (*UK tr*) in top of 3-ch. Turn.

(4 granny sets, 2 dc (*UK 2 tr*), 2 ch sps.)

Row 4: 3 ch, dc (*UK tr*) in sp between first 2 sts, [3 dc (*UK 3 tr*) in next sp between granny sets] to next ch sp, [3 dc (*UK 3 tr*), 1 ch, 3 dc (*UK 3 tr*)] in next ch sp, [3 dc (*UK 3 tr*) in next sp between granny sets] to next ch sp, [3 dc (*UK 3 tr*), 1 ch, dc (*UK tr*)] in next ch sp. Turn.

(5 granny sets, 3 dc (*UK 3 tr*), 2 ch sps.)

Row 5: 4 ch, 3 dc (*UK 3 tr*) in first ch sp, [3 dc (*UK 3 tr*) in next sp between granny sets] to ch sp, [3 dc (*UK 3 tr*), 1 ch, 3 dc (*UK 3 tr*)] in next ch sp, [3 dc (*UK 3 tr*) in next sp between granny sets] to last 2 dc (*UK 2 tr*), skip 1 st, dc (*UK tr*) in top of 3-ch. Turn.

(7 granny sets, 2 dc (*UK 2 tr*), 2 ch sps.)

Rep Rows 4 and 5 until desired size.

Fasten off and sew in ends.

Solid Hexagon
– QUARTER

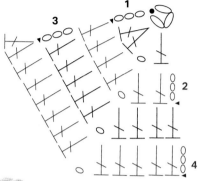

Skill level
Intermediate

Stitches used
ch, sl st, dc (*UK tr*)

Colour
Blush Pink

Symbol key

◄   direction to work

○   chain (ch)

●   slip stitch (sl st)

⊤   double crochet/
UK treble crochet
(dc/*UK tr*)

INSTRUCTIONS

3 ch, sl st into third ch from hook to form a ring.

Row 1: 3 ch (counts as dc (*UK tr*) here and throughout), into ring work 2 dc (*UK 2 tr*), 1 ch, dc (*UK tr*). Turn.
(4 dc (*UK 4 tr*), 1 ch sp.)

Row 2: 3 ch, dc (*UK tr*) in st at base of 3-ch, [dc (*UK tr*), 1 ch, dc (*UK tr*)] in ch sp, dc (*UK tr*) in last 3 sts. Turn.
(7 dc (*UK 7 tr*), 1 ch sp.)

Row 3: 3 ch, dc (*UK tr*) in st at base of 3-ch, dc (*UK tr*) in each st to ch sp, [dc (*UK tr*), 1 ch, dc (*UK tr*)] in ch sp, dc (*UK tr*) in each st to end. Turn.
(10 dc (*UK 10 tr*), 1 ch sp.)

Row 4: 3 ch, dc (*UK tr*) in st at base of 3-ch, dc (*UK tr*) in each st to ch sp, [dc (*UK tr*), 1 ch, dc (*UK tr*)] in ch sp, dc (*UK tr*) in each st until 1 st rem, 2 dc (*UK 2 tr*) in last st. Turn.
(14 dc (*UK 14 tr*), 1 ch sp.)

Rep Rows 3 and 4 until desired size.

Fasten off and sew in ends.

Corner-to-Corner (C2C) Granny Square

Skill level
Intermediate

Stitches used
ch, sl st, dc (*UK tr*)

Pattern note
A 'cluster' is 3 or 4 dc (*UK 3 or 4 tr*) worked in the same space.

Colour
Blush Pink

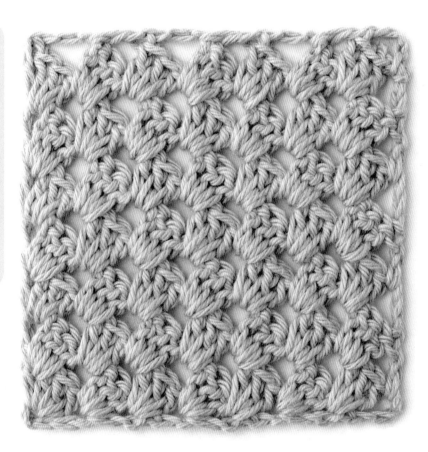

INSTRUCTIONS

4 ch, sl st into fourth ch from hook to form a ring.

Row 1: 3 ch (counts as st here and throughout), into the ring work 4 dc (*UK 4 tr*). Turn.
(5 sts.)

Row 2: 3 ch, 3 dc (*UK 3 tr*) in sp between first 2 sts, skip 3 dc (*UK 3 tr*), 4 dc (*UK 4 tr*) in sp between last 2 sts. Turn.
(2 clusters.)

Row 3: 3 ch, 3 dc (*UK 3 tr*) in sp between first 2 sts, skip 3 sts, 3 dc (*UK 3 tr*) in sp between clusters, 4 dc (*UK 4 tr*) in sp between last 2 sts. Turn.
(3 clusters.)

Row 4: 3 ch, 3 dc (*UK 3 tr*) in sp between first 2 sts, [skip 3 sts, 3 dc (*UK 3 tr*) in sp between clusters] to last cluster, 4 dc (*UK 4 tr*) in sp between last 2 sts. Turn.
(4 clusters.)

Rows 5–7: rep Row 4.
(7 clusters.)

Note: If you wish to make your square bigger, simply rep Row 4 until desired width. Note that the clusters will increase by 1 with each row.

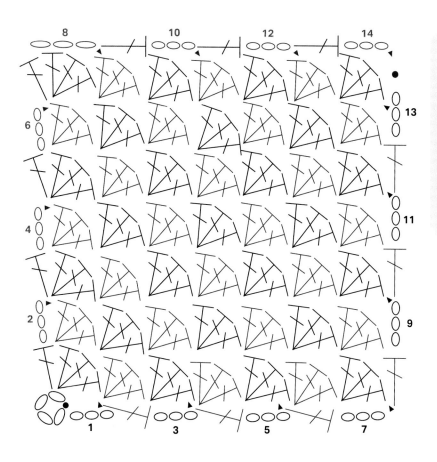

Symbol key

◄   direction to work

○   chain (ch)

●   slip stitch (sl st)

T   double crochet/
UK treble crochet
(**dc**/*UK tr*)

DECREASE ROWS

Row 8: 3 ch, [skip 3 sts, 3 dc (*UK 3 tr*) in sp between clusters] to last cluster, dc (*UK tr*) in sp between last 2 sts. Turn.

(6 clusters.)

Row 9: 3 ch, [skip 3 sts, 3 dc (*UK 3 tr*) in sp between clusters] to last cluster, dc (*UK tr*) in top of 3-ch. Turn.

(5 clusters.)

Rows 10–12: rep Row 9.

(2 clusters.)

Note: If your square is larger, repeat Row 9 until two clusters rem.

Row 13: 3 ch, skip 3 sts, 3 dc (*3 tr*) in sp between clusters dc (*UK tr*) into top of 3-ch. Turn.

(1 cluster.)

Row 14: 3 ch, skip 3 sts, sl st into top of 3-ch.

Fasten off and sew in ends.

Corner-to-Corner (C2C) Granny Rectangle

Skill level
Intermediate

Stitches used
ch, sl st, dc (*UK tr*)

Pattern note
A 'cluster' is 3 or 4 dc (*UK 3 or 4 tr*) worked in the same space.

Colour
Vanilla Cream

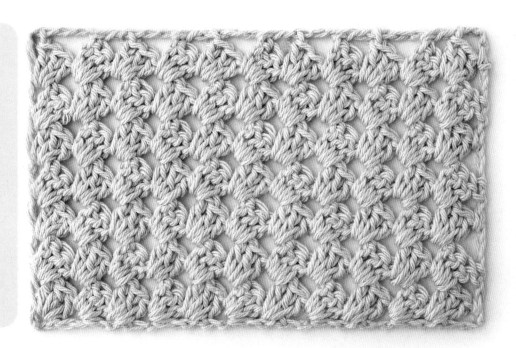

INSTRUCTIONS

4 ch, sl st into fourth ch from hook to form a ring.

Row 1: 3 ch (counts as st here and throughout), into ring work 4 dc (*UK 4 tr*). Turn.

(5 sts.)

Row 2: 3 ch, 3 dc (*UK 3 tr*) in sp between first 2 sts, skip 3 dc (*UK 3 tr*), 4 dc (*UK 4 tr*) in sp between last 2 sts. Turn.

(2 clusters.)

Row 3: 3 ch, 3 dc (*UK 3 tr*) in sp between first 2 sts, skip 3 sts, 3 dc (*UK 3 tr*) in sp between clusters, 4 dc (*UK 4 tr*) in sp between last 2 sts. Turn.

(3 clusters.)

Row 4: 3 ch, work 3 dc (*UK 3 tr*) in sp between first 2 sts, [skip 3 sts, work 3 dc (*UK 3 tr*) in sp between clusters] to last cluster, 4 dc (*UK 4 tr*) in sp between last 2 sts. Turn.

(4 clusters.)

Rows 5–7: rep Row 4.

(7 clusters.)

Note: If you wish to make your rectangle bigger, simply rep Row 4 until desired height. The clusters will increase by 1 with each row.

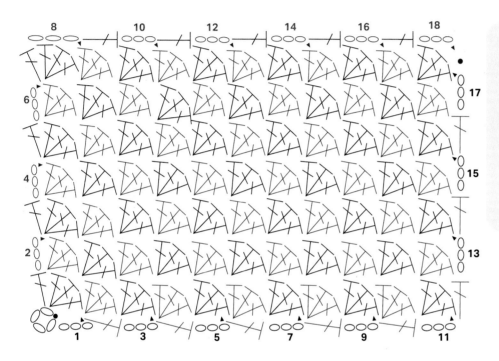

Symbol key

◄   direction to work

○   chain (ch)

●   slip stitch (sl st)

┬   double crochet/
     UK treble crochet
     (dc/*UK tr*)

ONE SIDE DECREASE ROWS

Row 8: 3 ch, [skip 3 sts, 3 dc (*UK 3 tr*) in sp between clusters] to last cluster, 4 dc (*UK 4 tr*) in sp between last 2 sts. Turn.

(7 clusters.)

Row 9: 3 ch, 3 dc (*UK 3 tr*) in sp between first 2 sts, [skip 3 sts, 3 dc (*UK 3 tr*) in sp between clusters] to last cluster, dc (*UK tr*) in top of 3-ch. Turn.

(7 clusters.)

Rows 10 and 11: rep Rows 8 and 9.

(7 clusters.)

Rep Rows 8 and 9 until desired width.

Row 12: 3 ch, [skip 3 sts, 3 dc (*UK 3 tr*) in sp between clusters] to last cluster, dc (*UK tr*) in the sp between last 2 sts. Turn.

(6 clusters.)

Row 13: 3 ch, [skip 3 sts, 3 dc (*UK 3 tr*) in sp between clusters] to last cluster, dc (*UK tr*) in top of 3-ch. Turn.

(5 clusters.)

Rows 14–16: repeat Row 13.

(2 clusters.)

Note: If your rectangle is larger, rep Row 9 until two clusters rem.

Row 17: 3 ch, skip 3 sts, 3 dc (*UK 3 tr*) in sp between clusters, dc (*UK tr*) in top of 3-ch. Turn.

(1 cluster.)

Row 18: 3 ch, skip 3 sts, sl st into top of 3-ch.

Fasten off and sew in ends.

V-Stitch Square

INSTRUCTIONS

4 ch, sl st in fourth ch from hook to form a ring.

Round 1: 4 ch, into ring work dc (*UK tr*) (4-ch and first dc (*UK tr*) counts as first v-st), 3 ch, *v-st, 3 ch, rep from * twice more, join with sl st into third of 4-ch. (8 dc (*UK 8 tr*), 4 1-ch sps, 4 3-ch sps.)

Round 2: 3 ch (counts as dc (*UK tr*) here and throughout), *v-st in next 1-ch sp, [v-st, 3 ch, v-st] in 3-ch sp, rep from * twice more, v-st in next 1-ch sp, [v-st, 3 ch, dc (*UK tr*), 1 ch] in last 3-ch sp, join with sl st into top of 3-ch. (24 dc (*UK 24 tr*), 12 1-ch sps, 4 3-ch sps.)

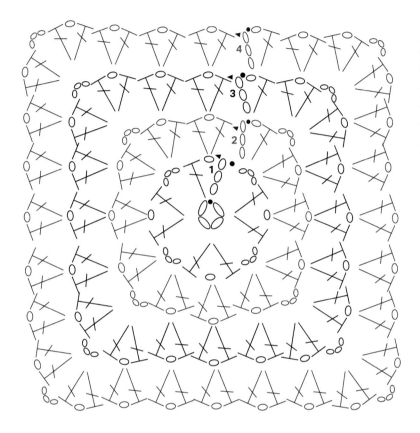

Symbol key

◄ direction to work

○ chain (ch)

● slip stitch (sl st)

† double crochet/
UK treble crochet
(dc/*UK tr*)

Round 3: 3 ch, *v-st in each 1-ch sp to corner 3-ch sp, [v-st, 3 ch, v-st] in corner 3-ch sp, rep from * three more times, [dc (*UK tr*), 1 ch] in last 1-ch sp, sl st into top of 3-ch.
(40 dc (*UK 40 tr*), 20 1-ch sps, 4 3-ch sps.)

Round 4: 3 ch, *v-st in each 1-ch sp to corner 3-ch sp**, [v-st, 3 ch, v-st] in corner 3-ch sp, rep from * three more times, v-st in each 1-ch sp to last 1-ch sp, dc (*UK tr*) in last ch sp, 1 ch, sl st into top of 3-ch.
(56 dc (*UK 56 tr*), 28 1-ch sps, 4 3-ch sps.)

Rep Round 4 until desired size.

Fasten off and sew in ends.

Circle in a Square

Skill level
Intermediate

Stitches used
ch, sl st, dc (*UK tr*),
hdc (*UK htr*), sc (*UK dc*)

Colours
Blush Pink (A), Vanilla Cream (B)

INSTRUCTIONS

Using yarn A, make a magic ring/adjustable loop.

Round 1: 3 ch (counts as st here and throughout), into ring work 11 dc (*UK 11 tr*), join with sl st into top of 3-ch. Close ring.
(12 sts.)

Round 2: 3 ch, dc (*UK tr*) in st at base of 3-ch, work 2 dc (*UK 2 tr*) in each st around, join with sl st into top of 3-ch.
(24 sts.)

Round 3: 3 ch, dc (*UK tr*) in st at base of 3-ch, dc (*UK tr*) in next st, *2 dc (*UK 2 tr*) in next st, dc (*UK tr*) in next st, rep from * around, join with sl st into top of 3-ch.
(36 sts.)

Round 4: 3 ch, dc (*UK tr*) in st at base of 3-ch, dc (*UK tr*) in next 2 sts, *2 dc (*UK 2 tr*) in next st, dc (*UK tr*) in next 2 sts, rep from * around, join with sl st into top of 3-ch changing to yarn B in last yo. Fasten off yarn A.
(48 sts.)

Round 5: 3 ch, dc (*UK tr*) in st at base of 3-ch, *1 ch, 2 dc (*UK 2 tr*) in next st, hdc (*UK htr*) in next st, sc (*UK dc*) in next 8 sts, hdc (*UK htr*) in next st, 2 dc (*UK 2 tr*) in next st, rep from * around omitting last 2 dc (*UK 2 tr*) on final rep, join with sl st into top of 3-ch.
(56 sts, 4 1-ch sps.)

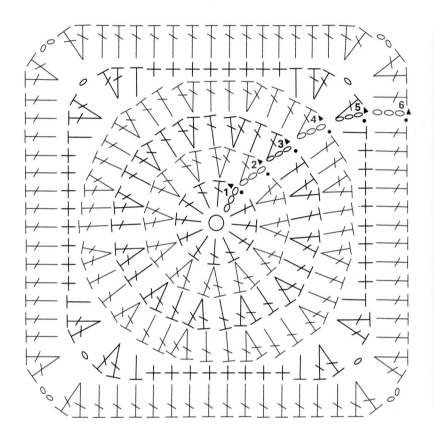

Symbol key

◄   direction to work

◯   magic ring/
     adjustable loop

◠   chain (ch)

●   slip stitch (sl st)

   single crochet/
├   UK double crochet
   (sc/*UK dc*)

   half double crochet/
┬   UK half treble crochet
   (hdc/*UK htr*)

   double crochet/
╤   UK treble crochet
   (dc/*UK tr*)

Round 6: 3 ch, dc (*UK tr*) in next st, *[2 dc (*UK 2 tr*), 2 ch, 2 dc (*UK 2 tr*)] in 1-ch sp, dc (*UK tr*) in next 14 sts, rep from * two more times, [2 dc (*UK 2 tr*), 2 ch, 2 dc (*UK 2 tr*)] in 1-ch sp, dc (*UK tr*) in next 12 sts, join with sl st into top of 3-ch.
(72 sts, 4 2-ch sps.)
Fasten off and sew in ends.

Bobble Circle Square

Skill level
Intermediate

Stitches used
ch, sl st, sc (*UK dc*), Beg-Bob – see 'Special stitches' below, Bobble – see 'Special stitches' below, tr (*UK dtr*), dc (*UK tr*), hdc (*UK htr*)

Special stitches
Beg-Bob = Beginning Bobble:
3 ch, [yo, insert hook in st at base of 3-ch, yo, pull through, yo, pull through 2 loops on hook] three times (5 loops on hook), yo and pull through rem loops on the hook, 1 ch to secure. The bobble will 'pop' out away from you

BobSt = Bobble variation:
yo, insert hook into next st, yo and pull through (3 loops on hook), yo, pull through 2 loops (2 loops on hook), [yo, insert hook into same st, yo, pull through, yo, pull through 2 loops on hook] three times (5 loops on hook), yo, pull through rem loops on the hook, 1 ch to secure. The bobble will 'pop' out away from you

Colours
Stormy Grey (A), Vanilla Cream (B)

INSTRUCTIONS

Using yarn A, make a magic ring/adjustable loop.
Round 1: 1 ch, into the ring work 8 sc (*UK 8 dc*), sl st in first sc (*UK dc*) of round to join.
(8 sts.)
Round 2: work a Beg-Bob in first st, [1 ch, BobSt in next st] around, 1 ch, 1 ch, sl st into top of first bobble to join.
(8 bobbles, 8 1-ch sps.)
Round 3: work a Beg-Bob in first st, 1 ch, BobSt in next 1-ch sp between bobbles, *1 ch, BobSt in top of next bobble, 1 ch, BobSt in next 1-ch sp, rep from * around, 1 ch, sl st into top of first bobble to join.
(16 bobbles, 16 1-ch sps.)

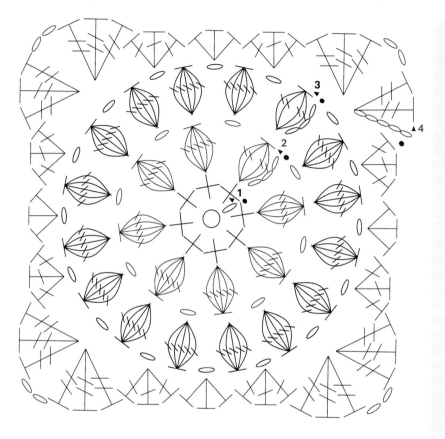

Symbol key

◄   direction to work

○   chain (ch)

◯   magic ring/
adjustable loop

●   slip stitch (sl st)

╫   single crochet/
UK double crochet
(**sc**/*UK dc*)

╥   half double crochet/
UK half treble
(**hdc**/*UK htr*)

╥̸   double crochet/*UK treble*
(**dc**/*UK tr*)

╥̿   treble crochet/
UK double treble
(**tr**/*UK dtr*)

◇   BobSt

Fasten off yarn A. Join yarn B into any 1-ch sp from Round 3.

Round 4: 5 ch (counts as tr (*UK 2 dtr*)), work [2 tr (*UK 2 dtr*), 2 ch, 3 tr (*UK 3 dtr*)] in same ch sp, *3 dc (*UK 3 tr*) in next 1-ch, 3 hdc (*UK 3 htr*) in next 1-ch sp, 3 dc (*UK 3 tr*) in next 1-ch sp, [3 tr (*UK 3 dtr*), 2 ch, 3 tr (*UK 3 dtr*)] in next 1-ch sp, rep from * twice more, work 3 dc (*UK 3 tr*) in next 1-ch sp, 3 hdc (*UK 3 htr*) in next 1-ch sp, 3 dc (*UK 3 tr*) in next 1-ch sp, join with sl st into top of 5-ch. (60 sts, 4 2-ch sps.)

Fasten off and sew in ends.

Block Stitch Square

Skill level
Intermediate

Stitches used
ch, sl st, dc (*UK tr*),
sc (*UK dc*)

Colours
Vanilla Cream (A),
Blush Pink (B)

INSTRUCTIONS

Using yarn A, either make a magic ring/adjustable loop (for a closed centre) or work 4 ch, sl st into fourth ch from hook to form a ring (for an open centre).

Round 1: 3 ch (counts as dc (*UK tr*) here and throughout), into ring work 2 dc (*UK 2 tr*), 3 ch, *3 dc (*UK 3 tr*), 3 ch, rep from * twice more, join with sl st into top of 3-ch. Fasten off.

(12 dc (*UK 12 tr*), 4 3-ch sps.)

Join yarn B into any 3-ch sp with a sl st.

Round 2: 1 ch (does not count as st here or throughout), [sc (*UK dc*), 3 ch, sc (*UK dc*)] in same sp, *2 ch, [sc (*UK dc*), 3 ch, sc (*UK dc*)] in next 3-ch sp, rep from * twice more, 2 ch, join with sl st into top of sc (*UK dc*). Fasten off.

(8 sc (*UK 8 dc*), 4 2-ch sps, 4 3-ch sps.)

Join yarn A into any corner 3-ch sp with sl st.

Round 3: 3 ch, work [2 dc (*UK 2 tr*), 3 ch, 3 dc (*UK 3 tr*)] in same sp, *1 ch, 3 dc (*UK 3 tr*) in next ch sp, 1 ch, [3 dc (*UK 3 tr*), 3 ch, 3 dc (*UK 3 tr*)] in 3-ch corner sp, rep from * twice more, 1 ch, 3 dc (*UK 3 tr*) in next ch sp, 1 ch, join with sl st to top of 3-ch. Fasten off.

(36 dc (*UK 36 tr*), 8 1-ch sps, 4 3-ch sps.)

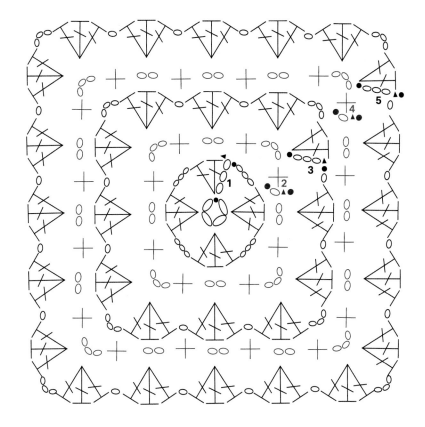

Symbol key

◄   direction to work

○   chain (ch)

●   slip stitch (sl st)

$+$ single crochet/
UK double crochet
(sc/*UK dc***)**

$\top$ double crochet/
UK treble crochet
(dc/*UK tr***)**

Join yarn B into any corner 3-ch sp with a sl st.

Round 4: 1 ch, [sc (*UK dc*), 3 ch, sc (*UK dc*)] in same sp, *2 ch, [sc (*UK dc*) in next ch sp, 2 ch] to corner 3-ch sp, [sc (*UK dc*), 3 ch, sc (*UK dc*)] in 3-ch sp, rep from * twice more, 2 ch [sc (*UK dc*) in next ch sp, 2 ch] to end, join with sl st to top of beginning sc (*UK dc*). Fasten off. (16 sc (*UK 16 dc*), 12 2-ch sps, 4 3-ch sps.)

Join yarn A into any corner 3-ch sp with sl st.

Round 5: 3 ch, [2 dc (*UK 2 tr*), 3 ch, 3 dc (*UK 3 tr*)] in same sp, *1 ch, [3 dc (*UK 3 tr*) in next ch sp, 1 ch] to corner 3-ch sp, [3 dc (*UK 3 tr*), 3 ch, 3 dc (*UK 3 tr*)] in corner 3-ch sp, rep from * twice more, 1 ch, [3 dc (*UK 3 tr*) in next ch sp, 1 ch] to end, join with sl st to top of 3-ch. Fasten off. (60 dc (*UK 60 tr*), 16 1-ch sps, 4 3-ch sps.)

Rep Rounds 4 and 5 until desired size, changing colour every round.

Fasten off and sew in ends.

Flower Hexagon

Skill level
Beginner

Stitches used
ch, sl st, sc (*UK dc*), Beg-Bob –
see 'Special stitches' below,
BobSt – see 'Special stitches'
below, dc (*UK tr*)

Special stitches
Beg-Bob = Beginning Bobble: 3-
ch, [yo, insert hook in st at base
of 3-ch, yo, pull through, yo, pull
through 2 loops on hook] three
times (5 loops on hook), yo and
pull through rem loops on the
hook, 1 ch to secure. The bobble
will 'pop' out away from you

BobSt: yo, insert hook into next st,
yo and pull through (3 loops
on hook), yo, pull through 2 loops
(2 loops on hook), [yo, insert hook
into same st, yo, pull through,
yo, pull through 2 loops on hook]
three times (5 loops on hook), yo,
pull through rem loops on the
hook, 1 ch to secure. The bobble
will 'pop' out away from you

Colours
Blush Pink (A), Vanilla Cream (B)

Symbol key

◄   direction to work

⬭   chain (ch)

●   slip stitch (sl st)

╪   single crochet/
UK double crochet
(sc/*UK dc*)

╪   double crochet/
UK treble crochet
(dc/*UK tr*)

⬭   BobSt

INSTRUCTIONS

With yarn A, 6 ch, sl st in first ch to form a ring.

Round 1: 1 ch (does not count as st), work 12 sc (*UK 12 dc*) in circle, sl st in first sc (*UK dc*) to join.

(12 sts.)

Round 2: work a Beg-Bob in first st, *5 ch, skip next sc (*UK dc*), BobSt in next sc (*UK dc*), rep from * four times, 5 ch, sl st into top of Beg-Bob. Fasten off.

(6 bobbles, 6 5-ch sps.)

Join yarn B in top of any bobble from Round 2.

Round 3: 5 ch (counts as dc (*UK tr*) and 2 ch), dc (*UK tr*) in same st, *5 dc (*UK 5 tr*) in next ch sp, [dc (*UK tr*), 2 ch, dc (*UK tr*)] in top of next bobble], rep from * four times, 5 dc (*UK 5 tr*) in last ch sp, sl st into third of 5-ch.

(42 sts, 6 2-ch sps.)

Fasten off and sew in ends.

Mitred Granny Square

Skill level
Intermediate

Stitches used
ch, sl st, dc (*UK tr*)

Colours
Vanilla Cream (A), Blush Pink (B),
Pistachio Green (C)

INSTRUCTIONS

With yarn A, either make a magic ring/adjustable loop (for a closed centre) or work 4 ch, sl st into fourth ch from hook to form a ring (for an open centre).

Round 1 (RS): 3 ch (counts as dc (*UK tr*) here and throughout), into ring work 2 dc (*UK 2 tr*), 2 ch, [3 dc (*UK 3 tr*), 2 ch] three times, join with sl st into top of 3-ch. Turn.

(12 dc (*UK 12 tr*), 4 2-ch sps.)

Round 2 (WS): 3 ch, 2 dc (*UK 2 tr*) into 2-ch sp, 1 ch, *[3 dc (*UK 3 tr*), 2 ch, 3 dc (*UK 3 tr*)] into next 2-ch sp, 1 ch, rep from * twice more, 3 dc (*UK 3 tr*) into next 2-ch sp (same sp as 3-ch and first 2 dc (*UK 2 tr*)), 2 ch, join with sl st into top of 3-ch. Fasten off yarn. Turn.

(24 dc (*UK 24 tr*), 4 1-ch sps, 4 2-ch sps.)

Join yarn B into any corner 2-ch sp with sl st.

Mitre Row 1 (RS): *(starting point indicated by '3' on chart)*
3 ch, 2 dc (*UK 2 tr*) into same 2-ch sp, 1 ch, 3 dc (*UK 3 tr*) into next 1-ch sp, 1 ch, [3 dc (*UK 3 tr*), 2 ch, 3 dc (*UK 3 tr*)] into corner 2-ch sp, 1 ch, 3 dc (*UK 3 tr*) in next ch sp, 1 ch, 3 dc (*UK 3 tr*) in next corner 2-ch sp. Leave remaining sts unworked. Turn.

(18 dc (*UK 18 tr*), 4 1-ch sps, 1 2-ch sp.)

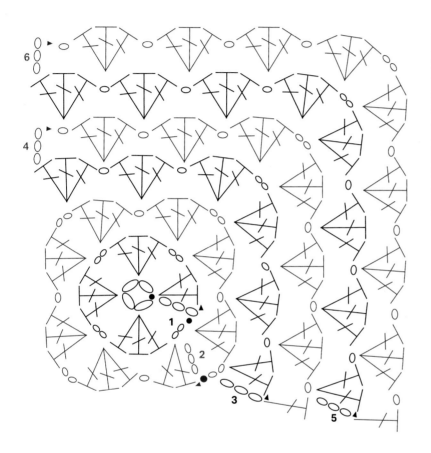

Symbol key

◄   direction to work

○   chain (ch)

●   slip stitch (sl st)

┬   double crochet/
      UK treble crochet
      (dc/*UK tr*)

Mitre Row 2 (WS): *(starting point indicated by '4' on chart)*
4 ch (counts as dc (*UK tr*) and 1 ch here and throughout),
[3 dc (*UK 3 tr*) into next 1-ch sp, 1 ch] to corner 2-ch sp,
[3 dc (*UK 3 tr*), 2 ch, 3 dc (*UK 3 tr*)] into 2-ch sp, 1 ch, [3 dc
(*UK 3 tr*) into next 1-ch sp, 1 ch] to end, dc (*UK tr*) in top of
3-ch. Fasten off yarn. Turn.
(20 dc (*UK 20 tr*), 6 1-ch sps, 1 2-ch sp.)
Join yarn C into final 1-ch sp from previous row with sl st.
Mitre Row 3: *(starting point indicated by '5' on chart)*
3 ch, 2 dc (*UK 2 tr*) in 1-ch sp, 1 ch, [3 dc (*UK 3 tr*) into
next 1-ch sp, 1 ch] to corner 2-ch sp, [3 dc (*UK 3 tr*), 2 ch,
3 dc (*UK 3 tr*)] into corner 2-ch sp, 1 ch, [3 dc (*UK 3 tr*) into
next 1-ch sp, 1 ch] to end, 3 dc (*UK 3 tr*) in last ch sp. Turn.
(24 dc (*UK 24 tr*), 6 1-ch sps, 1 2-ch sp.)

Mitre Row 4: *(starting point indicated by '6' on chart)*
4 ch, [3 dc (*UK 3 tr*) into next 1-ch sp, 1 ch] to next
corner 2-ch sp, [3 dc (*UK 3 tr*), 2 ch, 3 dc (*UK 3 tr*)] into
2-ch sp, 1 ch, [3 dc (*UK 3 tr*) into next 1-ch sp, 1 ch] to
end, dc (*UK tr*) into top of 3-ch. Fasten off yarn. Turn.
(26 dc (*UK 26 tr*), 8 1-ch sps, 1 2-ch sp.)
Rep Mitre Rows 3 and 4 until desired size, turning work
after completing each row and changing yarn colours
every two rows.
Fasten off and sew in ends.

Solid Mitred Granny Square

Skill level
Intermediate

Stitches used
ch, sl st, dc (*UK tr*)

Colours
Pistachio Green (A),
Vanilla Cream (B),
Stormy Grey (C)

INSTRUCTIONS

With yarn A, either make a magic ring/adjustable loop (for a closed centre) or work 3 ch, sl st into third ch from hook to form a ring (for an open centre).

Round 1 (RS): 3 ch (counts as dc (*UK tr*) here and throughout), into ring work 2 dc (*UK 2 tr*), 2 ch, [3 dc (*UK 3 tr*), 2 ch] three times, join with sl st into top of 3-ch. Turn.

(12 dc (*UK 12 tr*), 4 ch sps.)

Round 2 (WS): 3 ch, [2 dc (*UK 2 tr*), 2 ch, 2 dc (*UK 2 tr*)] in corner 2-ch sp, *dc (*UK tr*) in next 3 sts, [2 dc (*UK 2 tr*), 2 ch, 2 dc (*UK 2 tr*)] in corner 2-ch sp, rep from * twice more, dc (*UK tr*) in next 2 sts, join with sl st into top of 3-ch. Fasten off. Turn.

(28 dc (*UK 28 tr*), 4 ch sps.)

Join yarn B in any corner 2-ch sp with sl st.

Mitre Row 1 (RS): *(starting point indicated by '3' on chart)* 3 ch, dc (*UK tr*) into same ch sp, *dc (*UK tr*) in each st to corner ch sp, [2 dc (*UK 2 tr*), 2 ch, 2 dc (*UK 2 tr*)] in ch sp, dc (*UK tr*) in each st to corner ch sp, 2 dc (*UK 2 tr*) in ch sp, leave rem sts unworked. Turn.

(22 dc (*UK 22 tr*), 1 ch sp.)

Mitre Row 2 (WS): *(starting point indicated by '4' on chart)* 3 ch, dc (*UK tr*) in each st to corner ch sp, [2 dc (*UK 2 tr*), 2 ch, 2 dc (*UK 2 tr*)] in ch sp, dc (*UK tr*) in each st to end. Fasten off. Turn.

(26 dc (*UK 26 tr*), 1 ch sp.)

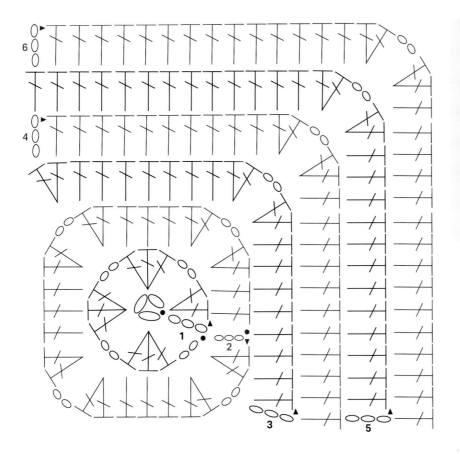

Symbol key

◄ direction to work

○ chain (ch)

● slip stitch (sl st)

⊤ double crochet/
   UK treble crochet
   (dc/UK tr)

Join yarn C in top of last st from previous row with sl st.

Mitre Row 3: *(starting point indicated by '5' on chart)* 3 ch, dc (*UK tr*) in each st to corner ch sp, [2 dc (*UK 2 tr*), 2 ch, 2 dc (*UK 2 tr*)] in ch sp, dc (*UK tr*) in each st to end. Turn. (30 dc (*UK 30 tr*), 1 ch sp.)

Mitre Row 4: *(starting point indicated by '6' on chart)* 3 ch, dc (*UK tr*) in each st to corner ch sp, [2 dc (*UK 2 tr*), 2 ch, 2 dc (*UK 2 tr*)] in corner ch sp, dc (*UK tr*) in each st to end. Fasten off. Turn. (34 dc (*UK 34 tr*), 1 ch sp.)

Rep Mitre Rows 3 and 4 until desired size, turning work after completing each row and changing yarn colours every two rows.

Fasten off and sew in ends.

BORDERS & EDGING

In this section you will find a selection of my favourite borders. You can add these to give a personal touch to your blankets, pillows and more!

Throughout this section, both US and UK terms are given – US is first, with the UK term following in italics and within round brackets.

WHAT YOU'LL FIND FOR EACH BORDER

Skill level: This will state whether it's classed as beginner, intermediate or advanced. Please note that this is just a guide. I'd always encourage you to give any border pattern a go!

Multiples: The multiple will be important when adding your edging, to ensure you have a balanced border design.

Stitches used: A list of stitches that are used within the overall stitch pattern. Refer to the 'Abbreviations' section on pages 171–175 to if you need to.

Pattern notes: These give you important information to help you create the border.

Instructions: These detail how to start, work the repeat and finish the border pattern, written in crochet shorthand.

Shell

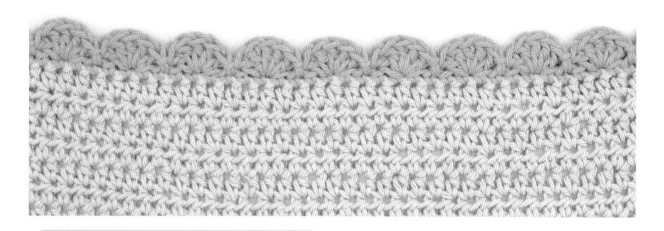

Skill level
Beginner

Multiples
4

Stitches used
ch, sc (*UK dc*), sl st, dc (*UK tr*)

Pattern note
The instructions are written with the assumption that you have completed your project, and are ready to add your border.

Colours
Blush Pink (A), Vanilla Cream (B)

INSTRUCTIONS

Note: if you need to adjust your stitch count so the edge of your work is a multiple of 4, you can sc2tog (*UK dc2tog*) – i.e. work 2 sts together – in one st at any point around the work in Round 1.

Round 1: with RS facing you and yarn A, sc (*UK dc*) evenly around the whole of your work, working 3 sts in each corner sp, join with sl st into first sc (*UK dc*). Do not turn.

Round 2: 1 ch (does not count as st), sc (*UK dc*) in first st, *skip next st, 5 dc (*UK 5 tr*) in next st, skip next st, sc (*UK dc*) in next st, rep from * around omitting last sc (*UK dc*) on final rep, join with sl st into top of first st.

Fasten off and sew in ends.

Wavy

Skill level
Beginner

Multiples
8

Stitches used
ch, sc (*UK dc*), sl st, hdc (*UK htr*), dc (*UK tr*)

Pattern note
The instructions are written with the assumption that you have completed your project, and are ready to add your border.

Colours
Blush Pink (A), Vanilla Cream (B)

INSTRUCTIONS

Note: if you need to adjust your stitch count so the edge of your work is a multiple of 8, you can sc2tog (*UK dc2tog*) – i.e. work 2 sts together – in one st at any point around the work in Round 1.

Round 1: with RS facing you and yarn A, sc (*UK dc*) evenly around the whole of your work, working 3 sts in each corner sp, join with sl st into first sc (*UK dc*). Do not turn.

Round 2: 1 ch (counts as sl st), *sc (*UK dc*) in next st, hdc (*UK htr*) in next st, dc (*UK tr*) in next st, 3 dc (*UK 3 tr*) in next st, dc (*UK tr*) in next st, hdc (*UK htr*) in next st, sc (*UK dc*) in next st, sl st in next st, rep from * around, join with sl st in 1-ch.

Fasten off and sew in ends.

Triple Picot

Skill level
Intermediate

Multiples
6

Stitches used
ch, sc (UK dc), sl st

Pattern note
The instructions are written with the assumption that you have completed your project, and are ready to add your border.

Colours
Blush Pink (A), Vanilla Cream (B)

INSTRUCTIONS

Note: if you need to adjust your stitch count so the edge of your work is a multiple of 6, you can sc2tog (*UK dc2tog*) – i.e. work 2 sts together – in one st at any point around the work in Round 1.

Round 1: with the RS facing you and yarn A, complete a round of sc (*UK dc*) evenly around the whole of your work, working 3 sts in each corner sp, join with sl st into the first st. Do not turn.

Round 2: *[5 ch, sc (*UK dc*) in st at base of 5-ch] three times in same st, 4 ch, skip 5 sts, sl st in next st, rep from * around with the final sl st being placed at the base of the beginning 5-ch.

Fasten off and sew in ends.

Camel

Skill level
Intermediate

Multiples
N/A

Stitches used
ch, sl st, hdc (*UK htr*)

Pattern notes
- The instructions are written with the assumption that you have completed your project, and you're ready to add your border.
- If you need to remind yourself of where the third loop is in your half double crochet (*UK half treble crochet*) stitch, see page 34.

Colours
Blush Pink (A), Vanilla Cream (B)

INSTRUCTIONS

With RS facing, join yarn A in any corner sp with sl st.

Round 1: 2 ch (does not count as st here or throughout), hdc (*UK htr*) in corner sp, hdc (*UK htr*) in each st across to the next corner sp, *[hdc (*UK htr*), 2 ch, hdc (*UK htr*)] in corner sp, hdc (*UK htr*) in each st to next corner sp, rep from * to beginning corner, hdc (*UK htr*) in first corner sp, 2 ch, join with sl st into top of first hdc (*UK htr*).

Round 2: 2 ch, hdc (*UK htr*) in corner ch sp (the 2-ch worked at end of previous row), hdc (*UK htr*) in third loop of each st across to next corner ch sp, *[hdc (*UK htr*), 2 ch, hdc (*UK htr*)] in corner ch sp, hdc (*UK htr*) in third loop of each st to next corner ch sp, rep from * to beginning corner, hdc (*UK htr*) in first corner ch sp, 2 ch, join with sl st to first hdc (*UK htr*).

Rep Round 2 until desired border width.

Fasten off and sew in ends.

Pompom

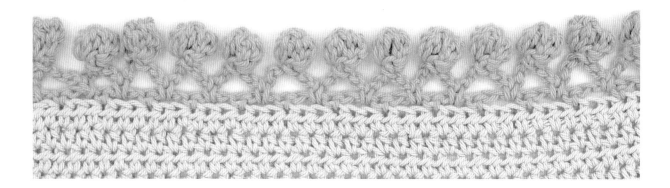

INSTRUCTIONS

Note: if you need to adjust your stitch count so the edge of your work is a multiple of 3, you can sc2tog (*UK dc2tog*) – i.e. work 2 sts together – in one stitch at any point around the work in Round 1.

Round 1: with RS facing you and yarn A, work sc (*UK dc*) evenly around the whole of your work, working 3 sts in each corner sp, join with sl st into first st (*UK dc*). Do not turn.

With RS facing, join yarn B n any corner st with sl st.

Round 2: 1 ch (does not count as st here or throughout), *2 sc (*UK 2 dc*) in corner st, 2 ch, skip 2 sts, [sc (*UK dc*) in next st, 2 ch, skip 2 sts] to corner st, rep from * around, join with sl st into first st. Turn.

Round 3: sl st into ch sp, *6 ch, PPst in third ch from hook, 3 ch, sc (*UK dc*) in next ch sp, rep from * around, omitting the final sc (*UK dc*) on last rep, sl st into st at base of 6-ch to join.

Fasten off and sew in ends.

Skill level
Intermediate

Multiples
3

Stitches used
ch, sc (*UK dc*), sl st, PPst – see 'Special stitches' below

Special stitch
PPst = Pompom Stitch: yo, insert hook into indicated st, yo and pull up a loop, yo and pull through 2 loops, [yo, insert hook into same st, yo and pull up a loop, yo and pull through 2 loops] twice (4 loops on hook), yo and pull through rem 4 loops on the hook. First cluster made. Make 3 ch, yo, insert into bottom of 3-ch at top of prev cluster, yo and pull up a loop, yo and pull through 2 loops, [yo, insert hook into same st, yo and pull up a loop, yo and pull through 2 loops] twice (4 loops on hook), yo and pull through rem 4 loops on the hook. Second cluster made. Fold second cluster down over the first then sl st into same ch first cluster st was made in, 1 ch to secure.

Pattern note
The instructions are written with the assumption that you have completed your project, and you're ready to add your border.

Colours
Vanilla Cream (A), Blush Pink (B)

PROJECTS

Faded Wrap

This wrap or shawl is made up of rhythmic stitches with a fun play on colour, making a gradient effect. Using a speckled yarn for the transition colour – the medium peach here – creates a subtle change between shades.

FINISHED SIZE

Approx. 16in (41cm) wide x 75½in (192cm) long

YARN

Hobbii Happy Place (Solid and Melange),
50% cotton/50% wool, light worsted (DK/8-ply/
weight 3), 3½oz (100g), 273yds (250m)

Yarn A: 2 balls in Solid 01 Almond
(beige)

Yarn B: 2 balls in Melange 07 Peach
(speckled peach)

Yarn C: 2 balls in Solid 07 Peach
(dark peach)

EVERYTHING ELSE

4mm (US G-6) hook

Yarn needle

Stitch markers

GAUGE (TENSION)

23 sts (counting sc (UK dc) and ch) x 19 rows
per 4in (10cm) square measured over Rows 1–3
of pattern using a 4mm (US G-6) hook

STITCHES USED

ch, sl st, sc (UK dc)

SPECIAL ABBREVIATIONS

PM: place marker in the indicated stitch

PATTERN NOTES

– Each of the three solid blocks of colour
has 104 rows. Each transitional section
covers 30 rows.

– For this pattern, each chain counts as a stitch.

INSTRUCTIONS

With yarn A, 93 ch.

Row 1: sc (UK dc) in third ch from hook (skipped 2-ch
counts as st), PM in top of 2-ch to mark first st, *1 ch, skip
next ch, sc (UK dc) in next ch, rep from * across. Turn.
(92 sts.)

Row 2: 2 ch (counts as st here and throughout), PM in
top of 2-ch just worked to mark first st, skip first
sc (UK dc) at base of 2-ch, *sc (UK dc) in next ch sp,
1 ch, skip 1 sc (UK 1 dc), rep from * across, sc (UK dc) in
top of marked st. Turn.

Rows 3–103: 2 ch, PM in top of 2-ch just worked to mark
first st, skip first sc (UK dc) at base of 2-ch, *sc (UK dc) in
next ch sp, 1 ch, skip 1 sc (UK 1 dc), rep from * across,
sc (UK dc) in top of marked st. Turn.

Row 104: rep Row 3, changing to yarn B in the last yo of
the last st. Fasten off yarn A.

Row 105: rep Row 3, changing to yarn A in the last yo of
the last st. Fasten off yarn B.

Rows 106–108: rep Row 3, changing to yarn B in the last
yo of the last st. Fasten off yarn A.

Row 109: rep Row 3, changing to yarn A in the last yo of
the last st. Fasten off yarn B.

Rows 110–112: rep Row 3, changing to yarn B in the last yo
of the last st. Fasten off yarn A.

Rows 113 and 114: rep Row 3, changing to yarn A in the
last yo of the last st. Fasten off yarn B.

Rows 115–117: rep Row 3, changing to yarn B in the last yo
of the last st. Fasten off yarn A.

Rows 118 and 119: rep Row 3, changing to yarn A in the
last yo of the last st. Fasten off yarn B.

Rows 120–122: rep Row 3, changing to yarn B in the last
yo of the last st. Fasten off yarn A.

Rows 123–125: rep Row 3, changing to yarn A in the last yo
of the last st. Fasten off yarn B.

Rows 126–128: rep Row 3, changing to yarn B in the last
yo of the last st. Fasten off yarn A.

Rows 129–131: rep Row 3, changing to yarn A in the last yo
of the last st. Fasten off yarn B.

Rows 132–134: rep Row 3, changing to yarn B in the last
yo of the last st. Fasten off yarn A.

Rows 135–238: rep Row 3, changing to yarn C in the last yo of the last st. Fasten off yarn B.

Row 239: rep Row 3, changing to yarn B in the last yo of the last st. Fasten off yarn C.

Rows 240–242: rep Row 3, changing to yarn C in the last yo of the last st. Fasten off yarn B.

Row 243: rep Row 3, changing to yarn B in the last yo of the last st. Fasten off yarn C.

Rows 244–246: rep Row 3, changing to yarn C in the last yo of the last st. Fasten off yarn B.

Rows 247 and 248: rep Row 3, changing to yarn B in the las yo of the last st. Fasten off yarn C.

Rows 249–251: rep Row 3, changing to yarn C in the last yo of the last st. Fasten off yarn B.

Rows 252 and 253: rep Row 3, changing to yarn B in the las yo of the last st. Fasten off yarn C.

Rows 254–256: rep Row 3, changing to yarn C in the last yo of the last st. Fasten off yarn B.

Rows 257–259: rep Row 3, changing to yarn B in the last yo of the last st. Fasten off yarn C.

Rows 260–262: rep Row 3, changing to yarn C in the last yo of the last st. Fasten off yarn B.

Rows 263–265: rep Row 3, changing to yarn B in the last yo of the last st. Fasten off yarn C.

Rows 266–268: rep Row 3, changing to yarn C in the last yo of the last st. Fasten off yarn B.

Rows 269–372: rep Row 3. Fasten off.

Weave in ends.

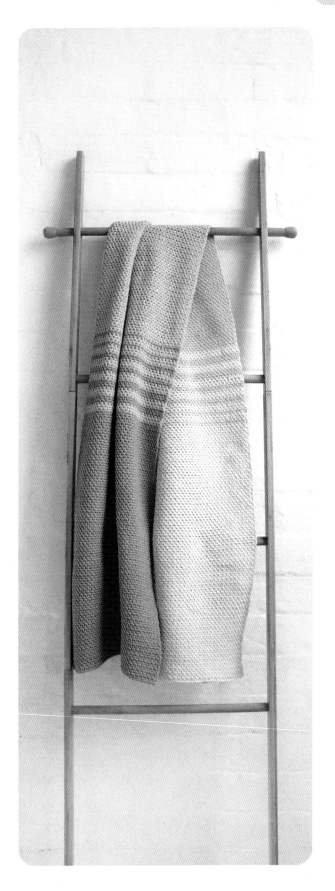

Fia Tote

The Fia Tote makes the perfect accessory to any outfit.
The beautiful mini basketweave texture makes for a modern yet
classic design.

FINISHED SIZE

Base of bag:
approx. 3⅜in (8.5cm) deep x 15in (38cm) wide

Bag side, laid flat and excluding handles:
approx. 20in (51cm) wide x 12in (30.5cm) tall

Bag side, laid flat and including handles:
approx. 20in (51cm) wide x 23in (58.5cm) tall

YARN

Lion Brand 24/7 Cotton, 100% cotton,
worsted (aran/10-ply/weight 4), 3½oz (100g),
186yds (170m)

4–5 balls in Ecru (beige)

EVERYTHING ELSE

3mm (US C-2/D-3) hook
Yarn needle
Stitch markers

GAUGE (TENSION)

21 sts x 25 rows per 4in (10cm) square
measured over sc (*UK dc*) rows using a
3mm (US C-2/D-3) hook

STITCHES USED

ch, sl st, sc (*UK dc*), hdc (*UK htr*), dc (*UK tr*)

SPECIAL ABBREVIATIONS

PM: place marker in the indicated stitch

PATTERN NOTES

– Refer to pages 172 and 173 for more information
on BP and FP stitches.

– You'll start by making the base of the bag,
followed by the sides. Your handles will be made
separately and then attached.

– Use stitch markers to mark each round,
moving up with each round.

INSTRUCTIONS

Bag Base

Make 81 ch.

Row 1: sc (*UK dc*) in second ch from hook (skipped ch does not count as st), sc (*UK dc*) in each st across. Turn. (80 sts.)

Rows 2–20: 1 ch (does not count as st here and throughout), sc (*UK dc*) in each st across. Turn.

You will now be working in rounds without turning the work. PM in the first st of each round and move it up for each round.

Bag Body

Round 1: 1 ch, hdc (*UK htr*) in each st across Row 20 of the bag base, rotate work 90 degrees to work down row ends and work 1 hdc (*UK 1 htr*) in each row end, rotate work 90 degrees and work 1 hdc (*UK 1 htr*) in the underside of each ch from the foundation ch, rotate work 90 degrees and work 1 hdc (*UK 1 htr*) in each row end, join with sl st into top of first st. (200 sts.)

Rounds 2 and 3: 1 ch, hdc (*UK htr*) in each st around, join with sl st into top of first st.

Round 4: 3 ch (counts as st here and throughout), dc (*UK tr*) in next st and each st around, join with sl st into top of 3-ch.

Round 5: 3 ch, FPdc (*UK FPtr*) around next st, BPdc (*UK BPtr*) around next 2 sts, *FPdc (*UK FPtr*) around next 2 sts, BPdc (*UK BPtr*) around next 2 sts, rep from * around, join with sl st into top of 3-ch.

Round 6: 3 ch, BPdc (*UK BPtr*) around next st, FPdc (*UK FPtr*) around next 2 sts, *BPdc (*UK BPtr*) around next 2 sts, FPdc (*UK FPtr*) around next 2 sts, rep from * around, join with sl st into top of 3-ch.

Round 7: rep Round 6.

Rounds 8 and 9: rep Round 5.

Rounds 10 and 11: rep Round 6.

Rounds 12–28: rep Rounds 8–11.

Rounds 29–36: 1 ch, hdc (*UK htr*) in each st around, join with sl st into top of first st.

Fasten off and sew in ends.

Handle (make 2)

Leaving a long tail, make 13 ch.

Row 1: working in the back bumps of the foundation ch, sc (*UK dc*) in second ch from hook (skipped ch does not count as st), sc (*UK dc*) in each ch across. Turn. (12 sts.)

Rows 2–8: 1 ch, hdc (*UK htr*) in each st across. Turn.

Rows 9–144: 1 ch, sc (*UK dc*) in each st across.

Rows 145–152: rep Row 2.

Fasten off, leaving an 18in (46cm) tail to sew with.

Assembly

Turn the bag inside out then lay one side flat in front of you. Measure 4in (10cm) in from each side of the bag (see the dashed arrows in **Fig. A** below), along the top edge, and PM.

Place the first handle over the bag side so that the short ends of the handle match the bottom of the hdc (*UK htr*) rows then *position the edge of one short end against the stitch marker. Using the long tail and a yarn needle, sew the handle to the inside of the bag (see **Fig. B** below).*

Ensuring that the handle isn't twisted, rep process from * to * with the other short end of the handle.

Turn the bag over to reveal the other side. Rep all assembly instructions from the beginning with the remaining handle.

Weave in all remaining ends.

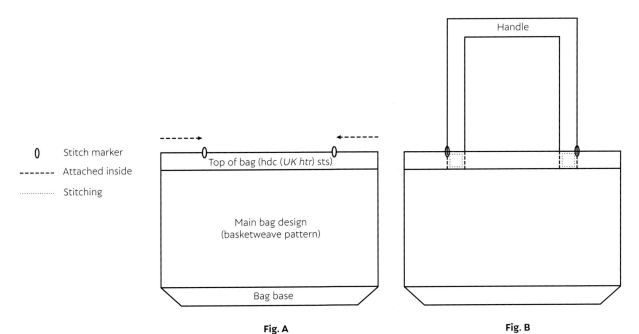

0   Stitch marker

------ Attached inside

.... Stitching

Handle

Top of bag (hdc (*UK htr*) sts)

Main bag design
(basketweave pattern)

Bag base

Fig. A

Fig. B

Florence Blanket

The Florence Blanket is a great way to explore stitches, and learn how to adapt different stitch multiples to make them work together.

FINISHED SIZES

Each blocked rectangle (before border): approx. 8in (20.5cm) wide x 9½in (24cm) high

Each blocked rectangle with border: approx. 9in (23cm) wide x 10in (25.5cm) high

Finished blanket: 46in (117cm) wide x 51in (129.5cm) high

YARN

Stylecraft Special DK, 100% Premium Acrylic, light worsted (DK/8-ply/weight 3), 322yds (295m), 3½oz (100g)

Yarn A: 2 balls in Duck Egg 1820 (mint green)

Yarn B: 2 balls in Blush 1833 (coral)

Yarn C: 2 balls of Pistachio 1822 (moss green)

Yarn D: 2 balls of Toy 1844 (peach)

Yarn E: 2 balls of Parma Violet 1724 (lilac)

Yarn F: 3 balls of Cream 1005 (off-white)

EVERYTHING ELSE

4mm (US G-6) and 5mm (US H-8) hooks

Yarn needle

Stitch markers

GAUGE (TENSION)

As this pattern is using multiple stitches, you need to make sure all of your rectangles are the same size. See 'Finished sizes' for details. Take a look at the chapter on pages 20–21 too.

STITCHES USED

sl st, ch, sc (*UK dc*), hdc (*UK htr*), dc (*UK tr*)

SPECIAL ABBREVIATIONS

PM: place marker in the indicated stitch.

Ssc (*UK Sdc*): Standing Single Crochet (*UK Standing Double Crochet*); see also page 174

CS: Cluster Stitch; see also page 172

HBdc (*UK HBtr*): Double Crochet Herringbone (*UK Treble Crochet Herringbone*); see also page 173

PATTERN NOTES

– Refer to pages 172 and 173 for more information on BLO and FLO stitches.

– When working rectangles, use a stitch marker to mark the first stitch of each row to avoid increasing or decreasing your stitches.

– Start by making all of your rectangles and then block them to the stated size. Then add the borders to each one, following the pattern.

– Block your rectangles once you have joined them and before you add the final border. This will flatten the seams and create a neat finish.

INSTRUCTIONS

Rectangles

Cluster Rectangle

Note: make one each in yarns A, B, C, D and E to make 5 rectangles.

Using a 4mm (US G-6) hook, make 38 ch.

Row 1 (RS): sc (*UK dc*) in second ch from hook (skipped ch does not count as st), sc (*UK dc*) in next ch, *1 ch, skip 1 ch, sc (*UK dc*) in next ch; rep from * until 1 ch rem, sc (*UK dc*) in last ch. Turn.

(37 sts.)

Row 2 (WS): 3 ch (counts as st here and throughout), dc (*UK tr*) in next st, CS in ch sp, *1 ch, skip 1 sc (*UK 1 dc*), CS in ch sp, rep from * until 2 sts rem, dc (*UK tr*) in last 2 sts. Turn.

(4 dc (*UK 4 tr*), 17 CS.)

Row 3: 1 ch (does not count as st here or throughout), sc (*UK dc*) in first 2 sts, *1 ch, skip st, sc (*UK dc*) in ch-sp; rep from * until 1 CS and 2 dc (*UK 2 tr*) rem, 1 ch, skip st, sc (*UK dc*) in last 2 sts. Turn.

(37 sts.)

Rows 4–25: rep Rows 2 and 3.

Fasten off and sew in ends.

Even Moss Rectangle

Note 1: make one each in yarns A, B, C, D and E to make 5 rectangles.

Note 2: from Row 2, you will be working the sl st into the sl st from the previous row and the hdc (*UK htr*) in the hdc (*UK htr*) from the previous row.

Using a 4mm (US G-6) hook, make 36 ch.

Row 1 (RS): sl st in second ch from hook (skipped ch does not count as st), *hdc (*UK htr*) in next ch, sl st into next ch, rep from * across. Turn.

(35 sts.)

Rows 2–47: 1 ch (does not count as st), *sl st in next st, hdc (*UK htr*) in next st, rep from * until 1 st rem, sl st in last st.

Fasten off and sew in ends.

Floret Rectangle

Note: make one each in yarns A, B, C, D and E to make 5 rectangles.

Using a 4mm (US G-6) hook, make 34 ch.

Row 1 (RS): dc (*UK tr*) in fourth ch (skipped 3-ch counts as dc (*UK tr*)), dc (*UK tr*) in each ch across. Turn. (32 sts.)

Row 2 (WS): 1 ch (does not count as st), dc (*UK tr*) in first st, sl st in next st, *dc (*UK tr*) in next st, sl st in next st; rep from * to end. Turn.

Row 3: 2 ch (does not count as st here or throughout), dc (*UK tr*) in first st, dc (*UK tr*) in each st across. Turn.

Rows 4–27: rep Rows 2 and 3.

Fasten off and sew in ends.

Suzette Rectangle

Note: make one each in yarns A, B, C, D and E to make 5 rectangles.

Using a 4mm (US G-6) hook, make 34 ch.

Row 1 (RS): [sc (*UK dc*), dc (*UK tr*)] in second ch from hook (skipped ch does not count as st), skip next ch, *[sc (*UK dc*), dc (*UK tr*)] in next ch, skip next ch, rep from * until 1 ch rem, dc (*UK tr*) in last ch. Turn. (33 sts.)

Rows 2–31: 1 ch (does not count as st here or throughout), [sc (*UK dc*), dc (*UK tr*)] in first st, skip 1 st, *[sc (*UK dc*), dc (*UK tr*)] in next st, skip 1 st, rep from * until 1 st rem, sc (*UK dc*) in last st.

Fasten off and sew in ends.

Herringbone Rectangle

Note: make one each in yarns A, B, C, D and E to make 5 rectangles.

Using a 4mm (US G-6) hook, make 32 ch.

Row 1 (RS): HBdc (*UK HBtr*) in third ch from hook (skipped 2-ch counts as hdc (*UK htr*)), HBdc (*UK HBtr*) in each ch across until 1 ch rem, hdc (*UK htr*) in last st. Turn. (31 sts.)

Rows 2–22: 2 ch (counts as hdc (*UK htr*) here and throughout), HBdc (*UK HBtr*) in each st across until 1 st rem, hdc (*UK htr*) in top of 2-ch.

Fasten off and sew in ends.

Rectangle Border

Note 1: work this border into the outer edge of each rectangle, using a 4mm (US G-6) hook throughout.

Note 2: when working along top and bottom of rectangle, increase or decrease to obtain correct st count as necessary. Increase by working 2 sc (*UK 2 dc*) in one st; decrease by working two sts together – sc2tog (*UK dc2tog*).

Round 1: with RS facing, join yarn F with Ssc (*UK Sdc*) in first st of top edge of rectangle, work 31 sc (*UK 31 dc*) evenly along top edge to corner, [sc (*UK dc*), 2 ch, sc (*UK dc*)] in corner, rotate work by 90 degrees to work along row ends, work 38 sc (*UK 38 dc*) evenly along row ends to corner, [sc (*UK dc*), 2 ch, sc (*UK dc*)] in corner, rotate work by 90 degrees to work along bottom edge, work 32 sc (*UK 32 dc*) evenly along bottom edge to corner, [sc (*UK dc*), 2 ch, sc (*UK dc*)] in corner, rotate work by 90 degrees to work along row ends, work 38 sc (*UK 38 dc*) evenly along row ends to corner, [sc (*UK dc*), 2 ch, sc (*UK dc*)] in corner, join with sl st into top of Ssc (*UK Sdc*). (148 sts.)

Round 2: 1 ch (does not count as st), hdc (*UK htr*) in each st to ch sp, *[hdc (*UK htr*), 2 ch, hdc (*UK htr*)] in ch sp, hdc (*UK htr*) in each st to ch sp, rep from * twice more, [hdc (*UK htr*), 2 ch, hdc (*UK htr*)] in last ch sp, join with sl st into first hdc (*UK htr*). (156 sts.)

Fasten off and sew in ends.

Assembly

Joining Rectangles

Note: Fasten off yarn at the end of each column and row.

Referring to the layout diagram (**Fig. A**), you will be joining the rectangles in columns first (**Fig. B**) then in rows (**Fig. C**) – see the diagrams below.

Place the first two rectangles ('C' and 'S') WS together. Using a 5mm (US H-8) hook and yarn F, and working through both layers, sl st in first ch sp to join and then sl st into BLO of front rectangle and FLO of back rectangle (the two loops closest to each other) across to ch sp, sl st in ch sp.

Place the next rectangle ('F') over the 'S' rectangle, WS together, then rep the above process.

Rep the process with the remaining rectangles until you have made five columns of five rectangles.

Now, begin joining your rows. Sl st in the ch sp of first two rectangles, then sl st into BLO of front rectangle and FLO of back rectangle (the two loops closest to each other) across to ch sp. Sl st in ch sp then work over join made from joining columns and continue to the end.

Final Border

Note: For Round 1 of the final border, the corner ch sps where the rectangles have been joined will count as a st. This will leave you with 4 corner ch sps.

Using a 4mm (G-6) hook and with RS facing, join yarn A with a sl st to top-right ch sp.

Round 1: 1 ch (does not count as st here or throughout), hdc (*UK htr*) in ch sp, hdc (*UK htr*) in each st to next corner ch sp, *[hdc (*UK htr*), 2 ch, hdc (*UK htr*)] in ch sp, hdc (*UK htr*) in each st to next corner ch sp, rep from * twice more, [hdc (*UK htr*), 2 ch] in ch sp, join with sl st into first st.
(4 ch sps.)

Round 2: 1 ch, hdc (*UK htr*), *hdc (*UK htr*) in each st to next ch sp, [hdc (*UK htr*), 2 ch, hdc (*UK htr*)] in ch sp, rep from three more times, join with sl st into first st.
(4 ch sps.)

Round 3: 1 ch, *BLOsc (*UK BLOdc*) in each st to ch sp, [sc (*UK dc*), 1 ch, sc (*UK dc*)] in ch sp, rep from * three more times, BLOsc (*UK BLOdc*) in last st, join with sl st into first st.
(4 ch sps.)

Fasten off and sew in ends.

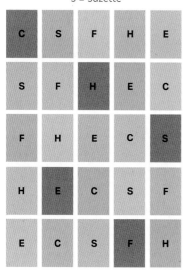

Fig. A: Layout diagram
C = Cluster
E = Even Moss
F = Floret
H = Herringbone
S = Suzette

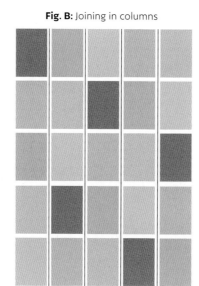

Fig. B: Joining in columns

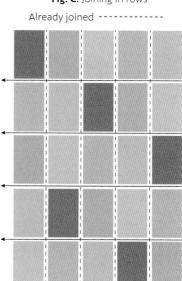

Fig. C: Joining in rows

Already joined - - - - - - - - - - - - -

ABBREVIATIONS

You will see a few abbreviations throughout this book, so let's bring them all together. American crochet terms are detailed first and prioritized on these pages; the descriptions contain the UK equivalents in round brackets.

( ) extra information or UK equivalent of stitch

[ ] work instructions within brackets as many times as directed

* or ** repeat instructions following the single asterisk as directed. If there are two repeats in a sequence, there will be a pair of asterisks

2tog 1 stitch decrease – the st you are working will be indicated at the beginning of this abbreviation: work the first st until the last 'pull through' of that st; then work into the next st until the last 'pull through', yo and pull through all loops on the hook

4tog 3 stitches decrease – the st you are working will be indicated at the beginning of this abbreviation: work the first st until the last 'pull through' of that st, * work into the next st until the last 'pull through', rep from * two more times, work into the next st until the last 'pull through' then yo and pull through all loops on the hook

Abs alternative bead stitch: [yo, insert the hook behind the previous dc (*UK tr*) from front to back, yo and pull through a loop] three times around the same dc (*UK tr*) (7 loops on hook), yo and pull through rem 7 loops

AS arrow stitch: yo twice, insert hook into st beneath previous ch sp two rows down from front to back, yo and pull through (4 loops on hook), yo and pull through 2 loops (3 loops on hook), yo and pull through 2 loops (2 loops on hook), yo twice, insert hook under next 1-ch sp two rows down from front to back, yo over and pull through (5 loops on hook), yo over and pull through 2 loops (4 loops on hook), yo and pull through 2 loops (3 loops on hook), yo and pull through the rem 3 loops

BAS backward arrow stitch: yo over twice, insert hook into st beneath previous ch sp two rows down from front to back, yo and pull through (4 loops on hook), yo and pull through 2 loops (3 loops on hook), yo over and pull through 2 loops (2 loops on hook), yo and pull through rem 2 loops

Beg-Bob beginning bobble: 3-ch, [yo, insert hook in st at base of 3-ch, yo, pull through, yo, pull through 2 loops on hook] three times (5 loops on hook), yo and pull through all loops on hook, 1 ch to secure. The bobble will 'pop' out away from you

Berry berry stitch: yo, insert hook into next st, yo and pull up a loop (3 loops on hook), yo, pull through 1 loop, yo, insert hook into same st, yo, pull through (5 loops on hook), yo and pull through rem 5 loops

BFS beginning feather stitch: yo, insert hook into first ch sp, yo and pull up a loop in line with loops on the hook (3 loops on hook), yo, insert hook into 1-ch sp or skipped st two rows below, yo and pull up a loop in line with loops on the hook (5 loops on hook), yo, insert hook in next 1-ch sp, yo and pull up a loop in line with loops on the hook, yo and pull through rem 7 loops

BLO back loop only: work st into only the back loop of the indicated st

Bobble bobble stitch: yo, insert hook into next st, yo and pull up a loop, yo and pull through 2 loops on the hook (2 loops on hook), [yo, insert hook into same st, yo and pull up a loop, yo and pull through 2 loops] four times (6 loops on hook), yo and pull though rem 6 loops on hook, 1 ch to secure

BobSt bobble stitch variation: yo, insert hook into next st, yo and pull through (3 loops on hook), yo, pull through 2 loops (2 loops on hook), [yo, insert hook into same st, yo, pull through, yo, pull through 2 loops on hook] three times (5 loops on hook), yo, pull through all loops on hook, 1 ch to secure. The bobble will 'pop' out away from you

BP back post: instead of working into the top loops of the indicated st, insert hook around post of st from back to front to back.

bst bead stitch: [yo, insert the hook behind the previous dc (*UK tr*) from front to back, yo and pull through a loop] three times around the same dc (*UK tr*) (7 loops on the hook), yo and pull through 6 loops, yo and pull through rem loops

CDC crossed double crochet (*UK crossed treble*): skip next st, dc (*UK tr*) into next st, dc (*UK tr*) into skipped st working over the previous dc (*UK tr*)

ch(s) chain(s): yo, pull through loop. If making the first ch for a foundation ch, make a slip knot before working ch

ch sp(s) chain space(s)

cm centimetres

CS cluster stitch: [yo, insert hook, yo and pull up a loop, yo and pull through 2 loops on the hook] three times, yo and pull through rem 4 loops

CThs closing thermal stitch: insert hook into both loops of next st PLUS the unworked loop on the row below, yo and pull up a loop, yo and pull through rem loops

dc double crochet (*UK treble crochet*): yo, insert hook into next st or ch, yo, pull up a loop (3 loops on the hook), yo, pull through 2 loops, yo and pull through rem 2 loops

Diamond St
diamond stitch: working around same st as the previous FPtr (*UK FPdtr*) or FPtr2tog (*UK FPdtr2tog*), work FPtr (*UK FPdtr*) but leave last 2 loops on hook, skip next 3 sts from two rows below, begin FPtr (*UK FPdtr*) around next FPtr (*UK FPdtr*) until there are 3 loops on hook, yo and pull through rem 3 loops

DPS double puff stitch: yo, insert hook into st, yo, pull through st and bring up to height of loop, [yo, insert hook into same st, yo and pull through st] four times (11 loops on hook), yo, pull through 10 loops on hook, yo and pull through rem loops, 1 ch to secure st

dtr double treble crochet (*UK triple treble crochet*): yo three times, insert hook into next st or ch, yo, pull up a loop (5 loops on hook), yo, pull through 2 loops (4 loops on hook), yo, pull through 2 loops (3 loops on hook), yo, pull through 2 loops (2 loops on hook), yo and pull through rem 2 loops

esc extended single crochet (*UK extended double crochet*): insert hook into st or sp, yo, pull up a loop, yo, pull through 1 loop only, yo and pull through both loops on hook

FAS forward arrow stitch: yo over twice, insert hook into st beneath previous ch sp two rows down from front to back, yo and pull through (4 loops on hook), yo over and pull through 2 loops (3 loops on hook), yo and pull through 2 loops (2 loops on hook), yo and pull through rem 2 loops

fc forked cluster stitch: yo, insert hook into the same st as last st made, pull up a loop (3 loops on hook), yo, insert hook into the next st, pull up a loop (5 loops on hook), yo, pull through 3 loops (3 loops on hook), yo and pull through rem 3 loops

FeS feather stitch: yo, insert hook into same 1-ch sp as last part of BFS or FeS, yo and pull up a loop in line with loops on hook (3 loops on hook), yo, insert hook into 1-ch sp or skipped st two rows below, yo and pull up a loop in line with loops on hook (5 loops on hook), yo, insert hook in next 1-ch sp, yo and pull up a loop in line with loops on the hook, yo and pull through rem 7 loops

Ffc first forked cluster stitch: yo, insert hook into indicated st, pull up a loop (3 loops on hook), yo, insert hook into the next st, pull up a loop (5 loops on hook), yo, pull through 3 loops (3 loops on hook), yo and pull through rem 3 loops

FLO front loop only: work st into only the front loop of the indicated st

FP front post: instead of working into the top loops of the indicated st, insert hook around post of st from front to back to front

fps foundation puff stitch: pull up a loop (around ¾in or 2cm tall), yo and insert hook into indicated st, yo, pull up a loop to the same height (3 loops on hook), yo and insert hook into same st, yo, pull up a loop to the same height (5 loops on hook), pinch first loop to secure then yo and pull through all 5 loops on the hook, insert hook into pinched st, yo and pull through (2 loops on hook), yo and pull through rem 2 loops

HBdc herringbone double crochet (*UK herringbone treble*): yo, insert hook into st, yo, pull through st and first loop on hook, yo, pull through first loop, yo and pull through rem 2 loops on hook

hdc half double crochet (*UK half treble crochet*): yo, insert hook into next st or ch, yo, pull up a loop (3 loops on hook), yo, pull through rem 3 loops

hdccl half double crochet cluster (*UK half treble cluster*): [yo, insert hook into st, yo, pull through] four times into next st, yo, pull through all loops on the hook, 1 ch to secure cluster

in inches

J-st jasmine stitch: pull up a loop (around ¾in or 2cm tall), [yo and insert hook, yo, pull up a loop to the same height] twice into top of last st worked (first puff st made, 5 loops on the hook), [yo and insert hook into next sp between puff sts, yo, pull up a loop to the same height] twice (second puff st made, 9 loops on the hook), [yo and insert hook into next sp between puff sts, yo, pull up a loop to the same height] twice (third puff st made, 13 loops on the hook), pinch first loop on hook to secure, yo and pull through all 13 loops on the hook, insert hook into pinched loop, yo and pull through (2 loops on the hook), yo and pull through rem 2 loops on the hook

LS   loop stitch: insert hook into st, wrap yarn around index finger and keep finger at desired distance from crochet (this will determine size of loop), bring hook over the top strand of loop around finger then catch the bottom strand of the loop to yo, pull through (2 loops on hook), carefully slip loop off finger and pinch it with middle finger to hold it in place, pick up working yarn with hook (being careful not to pull on the loop made), pull through both loops on hook to complete loop

m   metres

PM   place marker

PPst   pompom stitch: yo, insert hook into indicated st, yo and pull up a loop, yo and pull through 2 loops, [yo, insert hook into same st, yo and pull up a loop, yo and pull through 2 loops] twice (4 loops on hook), yo and pull through all 4 loops on the hook. First cluster made. Make 3 ch, yo, insert into bottom of 3-ch at top of prev cluster, yo and pull up a loop, yo and pull through 2 loops, [yo, insert hook into same st, yo and pull up a loop, yo and pull through 2 loops] twice (4 loops on hook), yo and pull through all 4 loops on the hook. Second cluster made. Fold second cluster over the first then sl st into same ch first cluster st is made in, 1 ch to secure

PS   puff stitch: insert hook into st, yo, pull through st and bring up to height of loop, [yo, insert hook into same st, yo and pull through st] twice (6 loops on hook), yo and pull through rem 6 loops, 1 ch to secure the st

PSt   popcorn stitch: work 5 dc (*UK 5 tr*) into st, loosen the loop on your hook then carefully remove hook, insert hook into top of first dc (*UK tr*) from back to front, insert hook back into the working loop (the one from which you removed your hook), pull the loop through the dc (*UK tr*) st

rem   remain; remaining

rep   repeat

RS   right side

Rsc   reverse single crochet (*UK reverse double crochet*); also known as 'crab stitch': without turning the work, insert hook into previous st from the last row, yo and pull up a loop, yo and pull through both loops

sc   single crochet (*UK double crochet*): insert hook into next st or ch, yo, pull up a loop (2 loops on hook), yo and pull through rem 2 loops

sc dec single crochet (*UK double crochet*) invisible decrease: this makes a neater decrease than the standard sc2tog (*UK dc2tog*). Insert hook into front loop of next 2 sts one after the other, yo and pull through (you will have 2 loops on the hook), yo and pull through both loops on hook

ScSt   scale stitch: work 5 dc (*UK 5 tr*) around post of the first dc (*UK tr*) of pair of dcs (*UK trs*) in previous row, rotate piece so it's upside down, work 5 dc (*UK 5 tr*) around post of second dc (*UK tr*) of pair of dcs (*UK trs*). One scale made

Ssc   standing single crochet (*UK standing double crochet*): with slip knot on the hook, insert hook into st, yo, pull up a loop (2 loops on hook), yo, pull through rem 2 loops

ShSt   shell stitch: work 5 dc (*UK 5 tr*) in indicated st

SK   Solomon's knot: pull up a loop to around ½in (12mm) tall, 1 ch, insert hook between the first and second loop of the 3 loops below hook and complete a sc (*UK dc*) (known as a closing sc (*UK closing dc*))

skip   to skip the indicated st. This can also be written as 'miss' (*UK preference*)

sl st   slip stitch(es): insert hook into next st or ch, yo, pull through st and loop on hook

sp(s)   space(s)

SpDc   spike double crochet (*UK spike treble*): dc (*UK tr*) into indicated st or ch sp two rows below

SpSt   spike stitch: sc (*UK dc*) into st or ch sp two rows below

SSp   stretched spike stitch: sc (*UK dc*) into st three rows below

st(s)   stitch(es)

SThs   starting thermal stitch: insert hook into BLO of next st PLUS the unworked ch on foundation ch, yo and pull up a loop, yo, pull through rem loops

TC   twin cluster stitch: [yo, insert hook into next st, yo and pull through, yo and pull through 2 loops on the hook] three times into the SAME sc (*UK dc*), skip the next sc (*UK dc*), [yo, insert hook into next st, yo and pull through, yo and pull through 2 loops on the hook] three times into the SAME sc (*UK dc*), yo and pull through rem 7 loops

Ths   thermal stitch: insert hook into BLO of next st PLUS the unworked loop on the row below, yo and pull up a loop, yo and pull through rem loops

tr   treble crochet (*UK double treble crochet*): yo twice, insert hook into next st or ch, yo and pull up a loop (4 loops on hook), yo and pull through 2 loops (3 loops on hook), yo and pull through 2 loops (2 loops on hook), yo and pull through rem 2 loops

TS   triangle stitch: yo, insert hook into first st as directed, yo and pull through (3 loops on hook), yo, insert hook into next st, yo and pull through (5 loops on hook), yo, insert hook into next st, yo and pull through (7 loops on hook), yo and pull through rem loops

v-st   v-stitch: work [dc (*UK tr*), 1 ch, dc (*UK tr*)] in indicated sp

WS   wrong side

yds   yards

yo   yarn over: bring the ball end of the yarn around the hook, from the front, in a clockwise direction. Sometimes known as 'yrh' (yarn round hook)

First published in 2025

Search Press Limited
Wellwood, North Farm Road
Tunbridge Wells, Kent
TN2 3DR, United Kingdom

Text, charts and diagrams
copyright © Sarah-Jayne Fragola, 2025

Crochet charts on pages 110–151 by Emily Reider

Photographs

Photographs on pages 110–151 by Mark Davison.
www.markdavison.com

All remaining photographs are by Nicola White.
www.bunnyandblossomphotography.com

Photography and design copyright
© Search Press Ltd., 2025

ISBN: 978-1-80092-219-8
ebook ISBN: 978-1-80093-201-2

Suppliers

Gauge swatch, techniques, stitches, shapes and borders on pages 20–157 of the book are made using Simply DK by Paintbox Yarns (100% acrylic DK, 100g/3½oz, 276m/302yds). Yarns used for projects are detailed within their respective patterns.

All the yarns in this book are available from www.woolwarehouse.com and www.hobbii.com

For details of alternative suppliers, please visit: www.bellacococrochet.com

Or the Search Press website: www.searchpress.com

About the author

For further inspiration, and for more information about Sarah-Jayne, visit:

– her website: www.bellacococrochet.com

– her YouTube channel, via @ bellacococrochet

– her Instagram page, via @ bellacococrochet

Measurements

The projects in this book have been made using metric measurements, and the imperial equivalents provided have been calculated following standard conversion practices. The imperial measurements are often rounded to the nearest ⅛in for ease of use except in rare circumstances; however, if you need more exact measurements, there are a number of excellent online converters that you can use. Always use either metric or imperial measurements, not a combination of both.

Bookmarked Hub

For further ideas and inspiration, and to join our free online community, visit www.bookmarkedhub.com

MIX
Paper | Supporting responsible forestry
FSC® C020056